Stand Together

A Collection of Poems and Short Stories for Ukraine

Contributing Authors

A.L. Butcher

Roman Nyle

Charles E. Yallowitz

Vickie Johnson

Andrew P. Weston

Rebecca Miller

Michael H. Hanson

Victoria Zigler

Richard Groller

KL Rhavensfyre

Joe Bonadonna

Anthea Sharp

Marta Moran Bishop

Colene Allen

J.C. Fields

Diana L. Wicker

Inge-Lise Goss

Sean Poage

Rebecca Lacy

Part 1 Poetry

The War That Was Not a War

A.L. Butcher

Never forget those who fell,
In a war which they said was not a war.

Never forget those who will fall,
In the war which is not a war.

Never defeated, never cowed,
In the war which was not a war.

Never broken, never afraid,
In the war which was not a war.

Never giving in to those who spilt blood,
In the war which was not a war.

A people stood, defiant, proud,
Against the war which was not a war.

The whisper became a cacophony,
Against the war, for it *was* a war.

Maybe Then

Roman Nyle (Marta Moran Bishop)

When the old are dying in the street
For lack of medicine and food
And babies are no longer being born
For your sons are off at war
Maybe then....

When the soil is tainted
With ash and soot
Chemicals beyond repair
And food cannot be grown
Maybe then...

When the air is unbreathable
For small or large
Creatures dying from lack of air
And the dead are lying in the streets
Maybe then...

When the water can no longer hold
Fish or fowl
So, polluted by mankind's waste
And not even from a bottle can it be drunk
Maybe then...

When the money is gone
For a debt called in
That cannot be repaid
And the government is laid to waste

Maybe then...

When the bombs start flying
Destruction everywhere
Children lying in blood upon the ground.
And life is nearly gone
Maybe then...

When the stores are empty
And there is no money left
You'll remember what your child said to you
When they called you on the phone.
Maybe then...

When your hospitals no longer
Have a decent doctor or nurse
For they have escaped Russia
For the west where they would be free
Maybe then...

When the jails are crowded with your children
Who protested the war in the streets
Sentenced to inhumane conditions
Because of the whims of a power-hungry madman.
Maybe then...

You will learn to open your eyes
To the propaganda around you
When all but the state-sponsored news is gone
You will finally see.
Maybe then...

You will hear the video of the Ukraine woman
Who confronted the soldiers, pushed sunflower seeds at them
So, when they are laid upon the ground
Sunflowers would grow where they once walked.
Maybe then...

What will it take to open your eyes
To the truth of your leaders lies
The bodies of your sons
Conscripted into service to die on foreign soil?
Maybe then...

Hope

Charles E. Yallowitz

Hope is necessary
And fragile beyond belief.

Hope fuels courage
And terrifies evil

Hope gives strength
To fight on and survive.

Hope is targeted by villains
To break spirits before bones.

Hope feeds bonds
Between those who stand together.

Hope is power
For the powerless and scared.

Hope is the light
Within all darkness.

Sunflowers

Vickie Johnstone

We think on a thing that's true,
talk of freedom, a reflection of the time
we cannot have, this yesterday of ours.
Boots stamp the hills of our country flat,
choke it with fire, wails and bullets,
black smoke, explosions splintering glass.
The snake rides its hide for 40 miles out,
carves a barren trench in our supple soil.

We hide inside our own shocked expressions.
This is not living. It's a smothering of life,
this sharp shock to the consciousness.
He walks with death, this stickman, the usurper,
this mad dictator whose greed is his undoing.
The old women weep. They hug our hearts
to their chests. We are rag dolls. Sunflowers
nod beneath a pale blue, quaking sky.

Where are the saviours? Where are our rescuers?
We ask for our skies to be sheltered,
but we are pleading to the silence of fear.
People fight and people tower ever higher,
growing in magnitude to match their courage.

The Science of Communication

Andrew P. Weston

The world is a stage of divisive alchemy,
A volatile mix of the reactive and repercussive,
Where conflicting belief and temperament,
Agitated in a medium of haste and inflamed passions,
Can only serve to stain the litmus of our hearts deep red.

Suicide bombings, gas and chemical attack,
Mid-air hijack, embassy storming and hostage taking,
Focus the lens of media hype intensely,
Warping it upon the acidic tendency to blame.
Where is the soothing balm of accord that might achieve so
much more?

Steel fist in velvet glove
May not always provide the most diplomatic or productive
solution,
Especially where a more discerning catalyst
May elicit a willingness to listen, to communicate,
To engage hearts instead of rhetoric.

Our challenge, therefore, is to foment a culture
Where both the desire and the willingness to act
Are synthesised within a framework of mutual accord and
justice.
We owe it to ourselves and to others.

Courage Personified

A.L. Butcher

The rage came on wings of fire
Sky-born and hateful.
Down, death-dealing on the street,
On babes, wailing into the world of fear
Born in blood, buried in rubble.

The rage rumbled, on feet of iron
Forty miles long and spitting mayhem.
Slow, inexorable, steel-clad,
Yet it quaked from the home-made fire
Thrown from grandma's hand.

The city stood, weary, disfigured.
Dark, hungry, filled with thirst.
Sandbags, barricades, the glint of defiance.
People ran, some hid, most fought in blood and dust
Bodies strewn, friend and foe.

The people trembled, shaken, bloody but unyielding
Death from above, death from all sides.
Their leader stood firm, never wavering
Heart of oak, balls of steel.
Courage personified – 'Raze us if you dare.'

The Sunflowers Will Rise Again

Rebecca Miller

I walked through the sidcyard of my house
Analyzing the dirt
Scattered seed pods, spikey, dried out, crushed easily under
my feet
The presently-desolate patch of earth on the border of my
presently-desolate patchy lawn
With a tall apple tree yearning for rain
My garden dormant
Spring is coming; I can feel it in my aged hands and feet
My youth in my past, my only child now a man
I stand in this desolate, barren space and hold my breath
And the sorrow brews in my chest, a heaviness
For the people of Ukraine.
My son, now in college, surrounded by his friends, had called
me in a panic
About the bomb
Their fear
Was my fear, but at his age, I watched the Berlin Wall get
torn down
And a country reunited
I listened to him on the verge of tears
Wondering what to do
I gave him my advice
Wisdom I'd hoped never to share
About bomb shelters, meet up spots, how to pack a go-bag
And the promise that if separated, I would find him. I would
never, ever stop looking for him
I reassured him that we had adults in the Office now

This has happened before
We will be ok
I told him to have hope; Spring is coming
He told me he loved me and hung up, feeling better
I had hope we'd speak again
I stood in my desolate patch of dirt and thought about the
other mothers
With their kids in college
And the bombs falling all around them
And the promise that they would never, ever stop looking for
them
Or the mothers whose sons went to war unknowingly
Would they ever see their child ever again?
Would hope be enough?
I stood on my barren track of land
And picked up my crushed pod
And shook its seeds free
Because I knew that once the rains come and the seeds are
absorbed into the earth
Despite the barrenness and the lack of rain
I had hope
My sunflowers will rise again
Hope
In rain and Spring
And resistance
The Sunflowers will Rise
The Sunflowers will RISE.

Wounds in Ukraine

Michael H. Hanson

The deepest wounds are in Ukraine,
raw ruptures in both flesh and earth
wrought by this age's darkest bane
granting young souls a dire breech birth.

Demons that fly assault the ground
as dragons belch horrific flames
and dazed fathers drown in the sound
of mothers grieving dying babes.

The shock and awe of invaders
releases a horrific rage,
slaughter is wrought upon raiders
whose blood now floods this savage stage.

Both hearts and souls succumb to pain
as plants and buildings nobly fall,
survivors oft envy the slain
no longer suff'ring Russia's gall.

Unfathomable however
this vast subterranean hurt
causes memory to sever
with hateful dreams none can avert,
lasting as long as forever
following spirits into dirt.

Civilized Humanity

Charles E. Yallowitz

We're so civilized
That's what humans think
But take a look around
There's disproof everywhere
Children getting beaten
Most animals aren't that cruel
People getting murdered
Raped
And robbed
We started out as savage brutes
But only one thing has changed
Humans still act like brutes
Though now
We all are bathed.

Shadows On Faces

Victoria Zigler

Shadows on faces
That should know only sunlight
Daytime terrors relived
In the dark of night.

A pair of gentle arms
No longer quite enough
To stop them seeing
That life can be tough.

Each briefly glimpsed
Moment of pleasure
Treated as fragile;
Worth more than treasure.

Shadows on faces
Who don't want to fight.

Where is the Line?

A.L. Butcher

When a thousand children die
Will you listen?
When ten thousand homes are gone
Will you relent?
When a million graves lie before you
Will you show mercy?
When the deaths of your people are at your hand
Will you cease?
When there is only obliteration left
Will you draw the line?

War Dance

Joe Bonadonna

The Dark King of Dreams mounted on his purple steed
Rode into the valley where the old dragons breed.
The Grim Wizard of Storms met him at their Holy Place
And there they did plot to destroy the Human Race.
The High Priest of Ashes called on the Gods of War,
While Trolls and Demons joined them, sailing from distant
shores.
The Scarlet Witch of Sorrow summoned forth her kin –
To the Lord of Worms they prayed, and offered gifts of sin.
Unicorns and Angels chanted in the dead of Night,
While Spirits rode moonbeams to bless their sacred flight.
The Prince of Solar Fire lit the beacons of his realm,
While trumpets blared a battle hymn – time to overwhelm.

The Sinister Snake winks at the Moon,
While stealing the eyes from the night.
Old unborn stars drown in the womb
Of a tapestry of Fright.
The Red Ghoul howls and growls at the Moon,
And keeps company with the Dead.
The remnants of Life are his to command,
And become one and all, his daily bread.

The Venerable Vampire spits a curse at the Moon during
intercourse with the Sleeping,
And the Children of Light writhe in dark Nightmare and
awaken to Shadows creeping.

The Wretched Old Rat shrieks at the Moon, while stalking
the alleys of Night,
And the Howling Hyena gnaws on old bones, and dwells in
cancerous Blight.

The Angel of Purity wears filthy wings,
The Angel of Death mourns and laughs as he sings.
The Puppets protest to the Marionette King,
While Destiny's Jester juggles all things.
The sky is burning and shedding its tears,
It mourns for the Living, who know only fear.
The deaf cannot see and the Blind cannot hear,
And only the Dead can rest through the years.

A Festival of Worms sings a hymn for Deformity's Children,
The hideous results of some ancient god's plan.
Blind are the sinners, Unfortunate Infants,
Crooked day morning where Specters now roam.
Awaken to Darkness, all silent and still –
On the Eve of Walpurgis you sleep all alone.
The King of All Fools lies drunk in the sand,
A goblet of hemlock still clutched in his hand.
The Children all flee from this creature of laughter
And mockingly call him the Halloween Man.
A crack in the Moon awakens the Sleeper,
Who sounds the Horn of Eternity.
The Echo of Thunder summons the Hunchback,
Who rings the Bells of Infinity.
Perverted Lepers preach their Unholy Creed --
That All is Nothing and Nothing is All.
Aliens in the graveyard applaud this grim sermon,
And Angels rebellious from Heaven now fall

Those Who Divide

Charles E. Yallowitz

They are the ones with voice
Born with a power
To influence and talk
Expected to lead us
Into the better world
But they always fall
Swallowed by the sins
Pride and greed
Vanity and wrath
They are twisted
By society's pull
Their voices turn to evil
Spouting hate and fear
Causing friends to fight
And families to splinter
Neighbors become enemies
They ignore their damage
Seeing only the faithful
The ones bowing at their feet
This praise is tainted
Grown from ignorance and terror
Yet it is not enough
Drunk off power from their voice
They become the great dividers
Crying for action
And hurling childish insults
At this who don't agree
Blindly building a void

A pit of animosity
Between our fellow man
Until the pit is all we see
And their putrid voices
Are all we hear.

Sorge*

Richard Groller

... and this is for the sorrow laden, grieving women,
always left as aftermath of war.

They, horror-struck, do beg and plead
that please, not theirs,
Oh No,
not their very own,
their sons and fathers,
their dear betrothed,
their life's mate 'til death do part
NO
do not go off to sure and sudden death
against a greater foe than man.

And still they go.
And still they beg.

Pity.
Pity.

Give them rest Oh Sorge!

For many, many have gone,
but few have returned whole.

* *From Goethe's* <u>Faust</u>, *the German word for Care, interpreted as one*
of the Three Fates from Greek mythology.

Ruins Hall

KL Rhavensfyre

Welcome all to Ruins Hall
Where colors bleed and fall to the ground.
Dripping lost words of distorted prophecy
And long drowned dreams.

Welcome all to Ruins Hall
Where concrete and steel boldly stand
A home for crows to stand in rows
A jury of nature's peers.

Welcome all to Ruins Hall
Where civilization crumbles and falls
False stones standing in homage
To mankind's failed ascendency.

Welcome all to Ruins Hall
Where the law abides on natures rules
Immune to our arrogant demands
To rearrange the universe.

Welcome all to Ruins Hall
Where the past decays yet refuses to yield
Rust oozing like blood of a mechanized grave
That we overly grieve for.

Welcome all to Ruins Hall
Where lessons are learned and passed along
Footpaths where we must learn to wander

In a forest grown from barren ground.

Lodestone

Andrew P. Weston

Whitewashed graves,
The true face of our world uncovered,
A people, whose moral compass,
Is still warped by violence and bigotry.

It doesn't take much for infection to take hold and spread.
A country of birth, an expression of faith,
The simple color of a person's skin,
Especially when hate has been fomented in the bile of rigid dogma.

Likewise, the jagged pill of hate,
Washed down with brain vomit from the masses,
Keep the seeds of malice germinating,
Ever ready to push through the cracks, like weeds.

Always insidious, ever vile,
Choking the life from everything decent,
While fanning the flames of intolerance,
That consumes society from within.

While there's still time,
Do you think society will be determined to make a change?
To keep the lodestone of their heart pointed true?
Or will moral lethargy keep strangling us to indifference?

The Vikings

Joe Bonadonna

Cast off the gauntlet and hang up the sword,
Tell our women and children we have conquered their horde.
Stoke up the hearth fires and break out the ale,
Listen now closely whilst I tell ye the tale . . .
They came out of the night to pillage and plunder,
The sound of their oaths was the roaring of thunder.
Through field and through forest they burned and they slew,
But the raiders were many and our warriors few.
Our enemies spread death as they swept through our land,
Spilling rivers of blood as we made one last stand.
They raped our young women and slaughtered the old,
Their crimes were too many to even be told.
But word quickly spread and our friends took up arms,
Coming to join us from towns and from farms.
We gathered together where the Vikings made shore,
They would pay with their lives, this we all swore.
We attacked them at dawn whilst they readied to sail,
We gave them a battle that made their hearts quail.
We kissed them with steel and embraced them with death,
No chance did we give them to even draw breath.
'Twas Erik the Tall who sounded the charge
And now he lies dead on the funeral barge.
But mighty was he and he held to his ground --
It took more than one foe to cut Erik down.
The sight of bold Ragnar riding off into doom
Filled me with pride and touched me with gloom.
His sword flashed like fire, dealing death to our foes,
But at last he was felled by their murderous blows.

And there, too, was Gunnar, swinging his axe,
He cut through our foes as if they were wax.
Then did he fall and was seen nevermore,
As down from Valhalla, Odin's tears they did pour.
I shall never forget the rage of that fight,
The cries of the dying still haunt me each night.
Many brave men lie in sweet endless sleep,
Like rain are the tears their families did weep.
The sun was a witness to that terrible day,
When good men were forced to fight and to slay.
The sky was a shroud that covered the Earth,
And each of us learned what a man's life is worth.
We fought 'til our arms were as heavy as lead,
We fought 'til the Earth was covered with dead.
When at last it was over and we stood by the sea,
I wept for my sons – those glorious three.
Now I pray that I die with sword in my hand,
Whilst fighting to rid our foes from our land.
I pray that I'm worthy of Lord Odin's praise,
When the Valkyries come at the end of my days.

Rape in Ukraine

Vickie Johnstone

This poem is about a protest in Tallinn against the rapes happening in Ukraine. On April 13, I read about a protest against rape in the Ukraine war in front of the Russian Embassy in Tallinn. The message of the organisers was: "Russian soldiers are raping and murdering innocent women and children in Ukraine. People who support this war also support war crimes, jarring murders to which they are accomplices. That is our message to the supporters of the Putin regime."

Hands tied, folded behind their backs
they stand dead still in a line straight,
half-naked, flesh exposed to the cold,
heads submerged in black plastic sacks,
because in war this is some women's fate,
and their horrific stories must be told.

In Tallinn outside the Russian embassy,
they show silent solidarity. They wait,
thinking of the women of Ukraine, so bold.
They protest the rapes we hear of on TV,
women murdered. Stone-cold.

Haiku

Joe Bonadonna

Artificial Intelligence
Robots won't serve man
We think, therefore we are gods.
Your time is over.

*

Haiku Uncertainty
Dystopian angst
No fate but the one we make
Future jeopardy.

Four Horseman

Rebecca Miller

I'd posted about how it seemed
How the four horsemen were arriving as the Scriptures
deemed
Staggered versus all at once
Like they were catching the Greyhound bus.

Pestilence, war, famine, death
COVID, Ukraine, grain exports eroded, what the F
Gen-X here, whatever, but my fear reawakened
Childhood threats of global thermal nuclear war left me
shaken.

You responded in the way I'd expected
As a selfish American MAGA hat wearing red
Massive school shooting 14 dead
But, my GUNS, you said.

Black Lives Matter protester gunned down not looting
Kyle is a HERO for shooting!
Masking mandate to reduce life lost
SOCIALISM!!! It's like the holocaust.

We attended the same primary school
where we learned the Golden Rule
Read the Bible, did math, colored pictures
We made sure to memorize the Scriptures.

We breathed fresh air

Rode the Zipper at the local fair
Spent sunny, muggy days at the pool
Eating chilled candies and trying to look cool.

We spent evenings catching fireflies
Under darkened, star lit skies
Over burning leaf barrels, we made s'mores
Never thinking about others of different shores.

We went on hay rides and Brownie Scouts
Our parents sent us on campouts
Our small town everyone knew each other
And we were minded by each other's mother.

Midwest raised
I left, you stayed

Suburban
Republican

Farmland
Reagan

White bread
Meat and potatoes fed

One Nation Under God
But not liberty and justice for all
Not for refugees taking flight
Unless not from shithole countries, only white.

I posted about the Four Horsemen and the instability of
Chernobyl
You laughed when I explained that my comment was global
You said our country was going to hell
I reminded you that the global wheat shortage affects you as
well.

Instead, you laughed
I said I was surprised
Really, I wasn't
I lied.

Because you gleefully cheered when kids were put in cages
And when Kyle shot the skateboarder
While your fearless leader rages
About the lack of law and order.

And Kaepernick is traitor
Kneeling for Black Lives being slaughtered
But you say Blue Lives Matter need protecting
Unless you're at the Capitol insurrecting
Then bear mace and fire hydrant beat downs now justified
And gouging out a police officer's eyes.

So why would it matter to you
When you have plenty of food
As you ease into a bed with soft sheets
It's the homeless man's fault he sleeps on the streets.

Everyone around you looks the same
Making it so much easier to blame
The Liberals for your discomfort

While you eat your white bread and mayonnaise smeared
liverwurst.

And whine about your gas prices
While driving your gas guzzling oversized truck
Not giving a fuck
About the children in Ukraine.

Who no longer slip into soft sheets
Or have bread to eat

No more safe days
Or quiet nights.

Eating s'mores
Catching fireflies

The bombs
fall
On the
children
Of
Ukraine.

We grew up together
We are not the same

Learning the same Bible passages
Such as, "I tell you the truth, whatever you did for one of the
least of these brothers of mine.
You did for me."

But you view people who are
brown/black/Muslim/queer/notwhitelikeyou as
SAVAGES.

But my gas prices are too high
my LATTE—the lines!
my gun rights—make haste
my Red Lining—voting restrictions can't wait!
Fearless leader Stop the STEAL!
Climate change isn't REAL!

All about me, mine, mine, mine.
Who cares about mass graves, we'll be fine
Those 400 civilians that were discovered
Fake news! Couldn't be bothered.

A six-year-old boy watched both of his parents shot dead
And you're bitching about the price of Wonder Bread

We shared the same teachers
Same friends, same preachers
What I hope is someday you might see
Humans around the world are the same as you and me.

With a love of smores
muggy days at the pool outdoors
of children and soft sheets
And white bread with a side of meat.

With a desire for peace as they make their way
Hoping for quiet nights and safer days

And to live freely as us here or perhaps stay
In the totally dysfunctional US of A.

Ukraine wants what we take for granted
The seeds of democracy long planted
We forget that our daily lives can be rearranged
As the GOP conspires to force regime change.

But since you'd like that, I unfriended you
No longer party to your glee seeped in hate—I've better things
to do
I finally rejected my parents' racist diatribes
With a city girl like me, your hate doesn't vibe.

All I know is that it makes me sad
When we can't muster sympathy for strangers in another
land
I do know that my love of God transcends
The mandatory high holiday show up under the cathedral
bend.

Doing the daily Classic Jesus thing
Without any attention or bling
Pray for Ukraine
Peace for Ukraine
Pray for peace for Ukraine.

Part 2 Short Stories

The Tree of Fate and Wishes

Anthea Sharp

Emer Cuinn woke from dreams filled with blood and ashes. Her parent's voices, low and urgent, penetrated the curtained-off sleeping area of their stone cottage. Emer lay still, straining to hear over the quiet crackle of the peat fire in the main room.

"What did the council say?" Emer's mother asked.

"It's to be war." Her father sounded weary. "We march to battle in four days."

Four days? Emer sat up, her heart racing.

"Already?" Emer's mother echoed her thoughts. "But Cormac, your wound...you cannot lead the warriors out."

"A chieftain leads his men into battle." His voice was hard.

"But your second—"

"Was Sean, and his replacement is still untested. Ask me no more. I'll not shirk my duty."

Sean, thought Emer, her bright and laughing cousin Sean, his merry voice forever silenced by a blade through his chest.

Careful not to disturb her sleeping siblings, Emer rose, the flagstones cold under her bare feet. Her mother alone could not convince her father, but perhaps he would listen to their combined voices. She wrapped a woolen shawl about her shoulders and pushed open the curtain, blinking in the lantern light. Her mother looked up from the table top, caution and hope in her eyes.

"Please, father," Emer said. "Can the battle not wait?"

Although the deep slice in Cormac's thigh was healing, it had sapped him of much of his strength. On the field of war, that weakness would spell his death.

"Those troublemakers graze their cattle upon our summer fields," he said, making a fist upon the table. "Already we've waited too long. We'll drive them off, and add their herds to ours. Which will add to your dowry, lass."

She did not want a dowry bought with the clan's lives. Especially not her father's life.

"We can move our cattle..." she tried again.

"These are our lands," her father said. "Ours by right of tradition. And force, if need be."

"Go back to bed." Her mother's eyes were sad. There would be no winning the argument that night.

Or any night.

Emer withdrew to the straw-stuffed mattress, but sleep did not come. The clan would go to war in four days. The words echoed in her mind, along with a rising sense of urgency. She must *do* something. But the chieftain's daughter did not have the power to command the clan, however much she might wish it.

Wish...

The thought sparked through her, and with it came a rush of hope. She could not change the course the council had decided upon, but she could invoke the old gods. They had the power to avert the coming war.

Some distance beyond the boundaries of her clan's territory lay a sacred spring. Above the spring a hawthorn tree grew, where for generations people had come to leave their wishes, tied to the branches in the form of cloth strips and long pieces of thread. In all seasons the tree was aflutter with color and movement, the cloth braiding and unbraiding in the wind, the strands dancing in the breeze.

At the wishing tree a girl could perform small magics, beseeching the powers to grant her heart's desire, whether it be love or vengeance or greed. Or peace.

Above the hawthorn tree rose a hill crowned with a circle of standing stones. It was a place of power, and peril. The old gods slept there, and the Fair Folk were known to dance in the ring. Any mortal who offended them brought trouble down upon her head, and upon her entire clan.

One did not go lightly to the wishing tree.

But go she must, for the specter of war panted at her shoulder—a wolfhound, fierce and insatiable, sharp teeth hungry for her father's blood.

* * *

The next day, once her chores were finished, Emer told her mother she was going to gather sweet herbs by the waterside.

"Don't stray too far," her mother said, giving her a stern look.

"I'll be careful." Emer fingered the small dagger strapped at her waist.

She collected her basket and, when her mother's back was turned, slipped an oat cake inside. One must always bring an offering to the gods when making a wish. Then she donned her blue cloak, kissed her brother and sister each upon the cheek, and set out.

At first she kept a decorous pace, but as soon as she was out of sight of the ring fort surrounding their village she gathered up her skirts and ran.

The sun shone down, the morning dew quickly drying from the grasses. The wind off the coast whipped her cloak back. She could not smell the sea—the shore and its tall gray cliffs were too far away—but she felt the weight of the ocean within the breeze.

When she tired, she slowed to catch her breath, then ran once more. She passed the stone cairn marking her clan's boundary and went more warily, though with no less haste. For a time swallows kept her company, darting and turning above her head, but when she came closer to the spring they flew away.

The wind calmed, too, and Emer spotted the weathered circle of stones on the hill above the sacred spring. She veered so she would not come too close to that circle, adjusting her path until the gnarled branches of the hawthorn tree came between her and the hill.

It was in full bloom, the flowers like snow upon the green thorns. Between the drifts of white she spied the colorful tatters of strips tied to the branches. Tens and tens of wishes, left to dance in the wind and flutter beneath the stars, sending their silent prayers into the world.

At the foot of the hawthorn tree the spring lay quiet and dark. A trickle of water wove around root and stone, finally gathering itself into a small stream and meandering away around the base of the hill. The air was thick with power and possibility.

Emer stood a moment, quieting her heavy breaths. She had run far and fast to reach the tree, but it would not do to approach it panting and disheveled. The old gods deserved more than that.

"Caw!"

She started as a raven took flight from the top of the tree. Guardedly, Emer watched it sweep across the sky. One raven was a portent, but not a dire one.

Stepping carefully, she approached the tree. No more dark shapes stirred in its branches. Still, she felt invisible eyes watching her, the weight of the place folding about her. Sunlight filtered through the hawthorn branches, laying patterns of light and shadow on the grasses.

"Greetings," she said softly. "I come with a peaceful heart to ask a wish."

For this, Emer was willing, though she knew it carried a cost.

She unslung the basket from her arm and drew out the oat cake laying her offering upon a flat stone near the spring's edge.

"Please accept this small gift," she said.

Her only answer was the breeze stirring the hanging bits of cloth tied to the thorny branches. Here, beneath the tree, the sweet dusty scent of the flowers filled her nose.

Sitting, Emer worked a length of blue thread free from the hem of her cloak. She snipped it off with her small blade, then brought the thread to her lips and breathed her wish upon the strand. Once, twice, thrice she whispered the words, blowing them against the thread until it was washed in the warmth of her breath.

"Let this war be averted. Let my father grow strong and well. Let us know a time of peace, not bloodshed, between the clans."

She looked up into the tree, finding a spot to tie her wish. Bees hummed among the petals, their song sharpening as they took notice of the large, clumsy human reaching in to disturb their work.

Though she was expecting it, the first sting on her hand made her yelp. Still, she did not withdraw, but looped her string about the dark wood of a small branch.

The second sting, this time on her finger, made her breath hiss between her teeth, but she tied the first knot in the thread.

The third sting was worse than the other two combined, landing in the center of her palm. Eyes blurred with tears, Emer could barely see to wind the thread about itself. Breathing hard, she finished securing her small magic to the tree.

The moment she let go, the wind lifted the blue strand, and her heart rose at the sight, despite the pain pulsing through her hands.

Perhaps Danu would hear her wish whispering in the breeze. Perhaps the Fair Folk would carry it to the mother goddess's ears. Perhaps all was not lost.

* * *

When Emer returned home, hands daubed with mud and a basket full of fresh herbs, her mother gave her a hard look, but said nothing. That evening Emer even had the heart to tease and sing with her siblings before the fire, and went to bed with a spark of hope in her heart.

Her dreams extinguished that spark.

The sky was full of ash, and the dead lay strewn upon the trampled grass. She walked among them, afraid to gaze upon their faces, tears scorching her eyes.

"No." Emer woke with a start, and clutched her blanket up to her chin.

One bit of magic was not enough. She must return to the wishing tree. Two more days, two more chances to strengthen the power of her wish before death came to eat them with its red, insatiable mouth.

I will avert this fate. She put all the force of her soul into the thought, holding it close until morning.

A new day, and warm porridge for breakfast, renewed Emer's resolve.

"Can I check the weirs for trout today?" she asked her mother.

Grainne gave her a long look, but finally nodded. "Keep out of trouble, mind."

"I'm not slipping away to meet with a boy, if that's what you fear."

"Hm." Her mother stirred the pot. "I saw the flowers Young Finn brought you last week."

Emer felt a blush warm her cheeks. "He'd given the same to Cait, the week before. I won't let the likes of Young Finn turn my head."

Though he was a handsome fellow. This last thought, however, her mother did not need to hear.

"Very well—but be home in time for supper. Especially if there's fish."

Emer kissed her mother on the cheek, then went to fetch her cloak and basket. This time, she tucked a small piece of honeycomb in alongside her oat cake.

As she had the day before, as soon as she was out of sight of the ring fort she ran. When she grew too winded she stopped at various points to catch her breath—the hollow where bracken fern grew, the hillock overlooking a rock-strewn plain, the thicket of thorny gorse.

At last, she came in sight of the hawthorn tree, the stone circle above standing sentinel. Clouds gathered overhead and the sun slipped behind them. The air suddenly carried a chill.

She paused to smooth her hair and catch her breath. Then, summoning her courage, she proceeded to the dark seep of the spring.

"I ask your indulgence again," she said to the spirits of the place, and to the old gods. "Please accept this offering."

She laid the cake upon the flat stone, and put the honeycomb beside it. Her wish for peace strong within her heart, she unraveled another length of blue thread from her cloak.

"Let this war be averted," she said. "Let my father grow strong and well. Let us know a time of peace between the clans."

The wish welled up from her heart. She could not bear to lose her father as they had lost Sean, now buried beneath the stones. Tears escaped the corners of her eyes, and she caught them upon the thread, letting her sorrow darken the strand.

A soft breeze tickled her cheek, as if in sympathy. Perhaps the gods *were* listening.

When Emer reached up to fasten her wish upon the branch, she drew in a startled breath and froze.

There, beside her first wish, was tied a length of red thread. Fear tickled the back of her neck, and she slowly turned, peering out from the shadows beneath the tree.

Was a warrior of the enemy clan lurking nearby, ready to run her through? Or worse yet, take her hostage?

As if her fright had called it forth, a raven burst from the branches overhead, cawing sharply. Emer's heart pounded like a drum, all her senses shouting at her to run—to abandon her wish and flee back to the safety of her own clan's boundary.

But no. Even if she was about to be taken, she must tie her wish to the tree.

As if from nowhere, a frigid wind sprang up. The air about her turned bitter cold, and Emer's breath plumed out in a white cloud before her face. Her fingers ached as frost swirled around them.

Moving as quickly as she could, she reached to the branch. It took several tries, her numb fingers more like twigs barely under her command than her own flesh, but at last a second blue thread hung beside the first.

The cold faded into a warm breeze and her wishes stirred, tangling and twining with the red thread: scarlet like blood, blue like the sky.

What did it mean? She shivered and backed away from the blossom-laden tree. A few petals blew down, dancing away in the wind.

And then she was away, too, running and running until she reached the cairn that marked the boundary of safety. Her hands still ached with a bone-deep cold.

It was growing twilight when she returned home, fingers chapped with cold, four fat trout from the weirs wrapped in leaves and tucked into her basket. Again, her mother gave her a hard look, but did not press.

After supper, Grainne and Cormac spoke of the coming battle, of the readiness of the clan's warriors, of the victory that must surely be theirs. The scrape of the whetstone as he sharpened his sword rasped against Emer's thoughts.

She lay awake, unwilling to fall asleep. When at last she did, ash and blood colored her dreams once more.

When she woke in the light of morning, her throat was clogged with unshed tears. Tomorrow the battle would come.

Almost, she gave up in despair. What good were her feeble wishes against the will of her father and the clan's council?

But stubbornness made her rise, and dress, and once more ask her mother if she might go out, this time to pick nettles.

"I want you close today," Grainne said. "The men are mustering, and the wind tastes of a blade's edge."

"Please." Emer's voice caught on the word. "I must go."

Three was a powerful number, everyone knew that. She must go one more time to the sacred spring, work her small magic, and tie her wish upon the tree.

"No." Her mother shook her head. "I need you to mind your siblings and keep them out from underfoot."

It was a request Emer couldn't refuse. And she would not take her brother and sister with her to the tree. Even if they could keep up, it was far too dangerous, especially with the evidence that someone else had been making their own wishes. Some enemy, wishing for her clan's downfall.

The sun crept across the sky, and Emer tended her siblings and the hearth, starting a rabbit stew and sweeping the floor. Late afternoon skimmed the sky with silver when at last her mother returned from helping provision the warriors.

"You've done well," Grainne said. "You may have your freedom until sunset—but stay close, and be home by dark."

"Thank you." Emer kissed her mother upon the cheek, hoping Grainne hadn't noticed her lack of promises to obey.

She would not be able to reach the sacred spring and make the return journey before twilight lay its shadow over the land. It would be well dark by the time Emer reached home, and she surely would face her mother's wrath, but there was no help for it.

She must make her final wish.

When Grainne wasn't looking, Emer tucked an oat cake into her pouch, along with a small bottle of elderberry wine. She bid farewell to her siblings, summoned a smile for her mother, and slipped out the door.

It seemed the land fought her as she ran—her skirt tangling in the gorse, her shoes sinking into an unexpected bog, thatched clumps of grass making her stumble. At last the hill above the spring rose before her, dark against the dusk-lit sky, the stone circle crouched atop it.

Emer picked the clinging burrs from her skirt and shook it out, then approached the hawthorn tree. A bird rustled in the upper branches, causing a drift of petals, but she could not make out what it was.

Please, not a raven. A third one was proof that the Morrigan, goddess of death and destruction, would bring war to the clan on the morrow.

But war was not a certainty, not yet. Clinging to that handful of hope, Emer laid her oat cake upon the flat stone. She was not sure if she should pour out the bottle of wine as a libation, or leave all the dark liquid within the bottle.

After a moment's hesitation, she unstoppered it and poured a small measure upon the ground, then settled the bottle beside the cake.

"I bring you my small offerings," she said into the oncoming night. "Please grant my wish."

The bird rustled once more among the branches, but still did not take flight and show itself. Afraid of what she would see, she glanced up to where her first two wishes hung.

A second red thread was tied beside her wish from yesterday, and her heart clenched

She stared at the scrap of red fluttering defiantly from the thorny branch. Anger flashed hotly through her. She wanted to turn and shout into the gathering twilight, demand that whoever was there show themselves. How *dare* the enemy come here and tangle their wishes with her own?

She should abandon her foolish hope for peace, and instead use her last wish for her clan's victory in the coming battle.

Emer closed her eyes, her heart torn. The memory of her cousin Sean's death rose within her, searing and futile. It would be easy to draw on that dark, bitter well of emotion, to push it into the magic and turn her hopes from peace to war. The third wish was always the strongest.

Hadn't the interlopers stolen their lands, and even invaded the sacred space of the wishing tree? Perhaps her father was right—the only way to respond was with force. Their warriors were brave and strong. With a heartfelt plea to the Morrigan, surely her clan would prevail.

But victory came with a price. She could not wish for her father to lie upon the field, dead face staring sightless at the sky.

When she opened her eyes, she saw that the first star had appeared, a speck of light in the ash-gray sky. It was a confirmation of what was in her heart.

Despite the darkest night, there would always be stars.

Tears pricking her eyes even as the star pricked the cloak of the sky, Emer unravelled a final length of blue thread from her hem. This time, after snipping it off, she did not sheathe her small blade. Her first wish had been imbued with her breath, the second her tears. Now it was time for her blood.

Hands steady, she set the tip of the knife against her thumb and pressed until a bright drop welled. Holding her wish close to her heart, she wound the thread about her thumb and let the blood seep in.

"Let this war be averted," she said, the truth of each word ringing from the bottom of her soul. "Let my father become strong again. Let there be peace between the clans."

In the silvery twilight, she reached overhead and fastened her wish to the tree. Her thumb throbbed and the thorns on the branch scored her hands, sharp and biting, as the wishing tree took its own blood sacrifice from her. Emer bit her lip against the pain and finished tying the knot.

The breeze sprang up, pulling the thread from her fingers to dance in the wind, braiding itself with blue, red, blue, red.

She withdrew her hands, the backs etched with burning scratches.

Above her, the bird took flight. For a moment all Emer could see was dark feathers, and her heart sank like a stone in deep water. A raven. A third raven. War and death would fall upon her clan on the morrow.

Then she caught a glimpse of white feathers among the black. As the bird flew away, the burbling call of a magpie reached her ears. She went to her knees in relief, the dampness soaking through her skirt, but she did not care.

She had done all she could. Now she must make her way home in the dark and face her punishment—hard words and a willow cane switching at the least. But if the gods and spirits heard her wish, it was a small price to pay.

Under the pale light of the stars and a sickle moon, she made what haste she could, but it was still two hours after sundown when she at last approached the ring fort.

"Who is it?" The guard at the gate lifted his torch, and she saw that Young Finn was on watch.

"'Tis I, Emer," she said wearily. "Let me in."

"Oh, your parents are sore," he said, standing aside. "What have you been up to, out there in the dark?"

He peered into the night, as if expecting to see she'd been keeping company with someone.

"Wishing," she said.

"For victory, I hope!" His smile was white and filled with anticipation. "Tomorrow will be a glorious battle. Give me kiss, for luck."

She brushed her lips against his cheek, but while his heart beat with red blood, hers pulsed with spring water. *Peace, peace.*

When she stepped through the door of their home, she was met with her mother's cold gaze, and her father's face set in anger.

"I know," she said, holding up her poor, abused hands. "I deserve whatever punishment you care to give me. But believe me that I have done what I had to do."

"To bed." Her father pointed to curtain wall, beyond which her brother and sister already slept. "Your punishment will come—but not this night. We must all rest and make ready for tomorrow's battle."

Emer bent her head and hurried to prepare for bed. Whatever befell her clan on the morrow, it was in fate's hands.

* * *

Emer awoke the next morning with no memory of dreams. Predawn light sifted in through the window openings, and she felt the first stirrings of hope.

Then she turned over and saw her father strapping on his boiled leather breastplate. So, the warriors had not all woken with their desire for battle extinguished.

Surely the gods would act. Her dreams had not carried blood and ash. Did that mean the war was averted?

Quietly, she rose and dressed. She went out and helped her mother serve the men, and few fighting women, mugs of hot herbal brew. Soon after, the warriors were ready, massing at the front gate.

Emer tasted bitter hopelessness.

"I am going with the healers," she told her mother, as the non-combatants prepared to depart with the fighters. When her father fell, she would be there to tend him.

"Emer, what—"

"I am going." She grasped her mother's arms. "I must."

Grainne's dark eyes studied her. Finally, she took her daughter's face between her calloused hands.

"Be careful," was all she said, though her expression was full of love and fear and questions that Emer could not answer.

Emer shouldered a pack of supplies and set out along with the healers. In front of them, the younger warriors called cheerfully to one another, while the older men, like her father, went grimly forward. They, at least, knew that battles brought death as well as glory.

Too soon they reached the field where the chieftains had agreed to meet. The sun had risen and clawed away the mist shrouding its face. It was far too beautiful a morning for death, and Emer swallowed back the salt of her tears.

At least she would be there to bear witness as her clansmen fell. Her heart hardened against the gods as she saw the black line of opposing warriors waiting across the field. There would be no peace.

Grief aching through her body, Emer set down the pack she'd been carrying. Despite herself, her feet carried her forward until she stood at the front lines.

"Get back," Young Finn told her, with a fierce look.

Then the war pipes began to play, wailing loud as though giving voice to her anguish. Across the field, Emer glimpsed a red cloak.

No.

She did not realize she was screaming the word as she sprinted forward. Open sky and green grass lay before her; and the faces of her enemies. Dimly, she was aware of a handful of warriors following behind her.

The opposing clan stirred, a group of them also moving onto the field.

"Come back!" her father called, but she could not.

There, as if in a mirror, a dark-haired girl in a red cloak ran across the field toward Emer, her face full of sorrow, full of hope. Behind her came her clan's warriors, until they were halted by a sharp command from their chieftain.

Closer Emer came to the stranger girl, closer, and closer still, until they met in the middle of the field.

"You," Emer gasped out. "You were wishing. Tell me—tell me, what was you wish."

"I wished for peace," the other girl said. "My name is Dierdre."

"I am Emer. And I wished the same." She could not keep a tear from slipping down her face.

"Well met, friend." Dierdre held out her hands.

They were welted with bee stings, chapped with cold, covered with scratches.

Emer stepped forward and clasped Dierdre's hands.

"Yes," was all she said.

They embraced then, and the breeze danced about them, whipping their cloaks together, red and blue.

Behind each of them, the warriors stilled and whispered. The chieftains waved their men back. Each one strode to the center of the field where their wayward daughters stood, hair tangling together, faces bright with hope.

The men halted beneath the gazes of their daughters. And their faces fell, and then rose as their eyes met. They began to speak, low and earnest. Then nodded, then a final clasping of wrists, before each turned back to their own.

There would be no war that day.

Nor was there, not for generations. Not until the last of the red thread and the blue thread frayed and faded and finally let go, whirling away from the tree into a night filled with wind, and stars, and the memory of two girls standing arm-in-arm against the tide.

The End

The Secret of Blossom Rise

A.L. Butcher

August 2015

Rain fell for the thirtieth consecutive day on paving that had needed repairing several decades ago and the sky was iron-grey. Smoke rose around two women sheltered beneath a large red umbrella. "When will it end? I'm sick of it," Georgina asked, grumbling as she looked around the rather tumbled-down buildings, and behind them, the remnants of a stone bunker now bedecked with Creeping Virginia and home to birds, and it was said a ghost or two. It was, everyone knew – out of bounds. Unsafe. The 'Keep Out' sign was rotten and unsteady, and the dark doorway used as an occasional haunt for the smokers. But most people avoided it. With the tumbling plants, with large leaves of blood-red the place had an eerie presence, yet strangely compelling, Georgina thought. Something about it made her wish to know more. In fact, that was the case with the whole hospital. Crater Hospital did not sound the most reassuring place in which to convalesce, but it gave good experience for nursing, and besides Georgina's friend was also working here. The nurse had found the bustle of the city hospital very draining, very demanding. She was a quiet spirit at heart, and Arabella had told her about the intriguing place.

"You'd love it, Georgie – quiet, easy-going and apparently, it's haunted. I know you like that sort of rubbish. There are a couple of positions here, and the turnover is high – but don't let that stop you. I know how unhappy you've been at Central." The emails between the two were regular, and Georgina found herself lonely and in need of a change since her long-time friend had moved to the country with her husband. She'd always felt rather rootless, and though a piece of her was missing, but never why. Places called to her, often the overgrown, remote and unloved or forgotten places and the city simply did not have the same call.

Google had told her the Crater Hospital was a kind, caring and friendly place, partly refurbished and the older part had listed status. There were gaps in the record. "Old military – I bet," She'd murmured.

It looked pleasant enough from the website and had a new psychiatric training suite. Georgina delved further – among the paranormal pages she visited. As with most information of such a nature, there was nothing concrete – occasional strange sightings, odd goings-on. But no one said much, it was a place largely forgotten about. There were better places to ghost watch.

"Work or this damn rain?" Arabella asked her, looking at the wet sky and grinning. "You've only been here a couple of weeks don't tell me you're bored already?"

"The rain. The job is OK. Odd place though, this. Don't you think? You said it was, but I wasn't sure at first." She relit her cigarette, "Full of ghosts."

Arabella shrugged, "If you say so. It's pretty old. That crater behind the bunker is full of water, and there's a wing that no one uses much. I guess everyone favours B Wing – that was only built ten years ago and is the bit the public sees. The rest is not often used – apart from occasional patients for Dr Horton's nut farm."

"Arabella! You know you mustn't call it that. It does look like something out of a film though. I feel at home here, lots of secrets. And some say it's haunted, of course."

"You know I don't believe in ghosts. People die and that is that. There is always a rational explanation." The two women had argued over this before, albeit good-naturedly. "Old hospitals always have a strange air. All those people who've died." She waggled her fingers and 'ooohed' at her friend. Arabella did not hold with ghosts, or souls lingering after death. She was far too practical for that.

"Sister Ramsey says it was a hospital in the war. But there was some secret stuff going on, you know like Bletchley or something. There was a tragedy here, but that was probably par for the course in military hospitals." Georgina gazed at the bunker door, finding she couldn't look away.

"Yes, I heard that. The crater was from a German bomb which fell. That's why it's called the Crater Hospital now – to honour the dead. It was Blossom Hill in the forties or something like that." Arabella stamped out the remains of her cigarette. "Come on we better go. Bedpans don't wash themselves, unfortunately."

"Blossom Hill? Are you sure? Could it be Blossom Rise?" Georgina had stopped in her tracks.

"Maybe, why what does it matter what the old place was called seventy years ago?"

Georgina shook her head. "I suppose it doesn't." Without another word she moved on, thoughtful.

* * *

"Mum, what was that place Grandpa Leo was at in the war?" Georgina asked on her weekly call to her elderly mother. She didn't often speak to her about the family now long gone. Her mother had grown up fatherless, and it was still a bit of a sore point, even after so long. Georgina's late grandmother had died many years ago, but the nurse remembered her as a proud, inflexible woman, who often talked about her own woes and sufferings. They had dwelled too long in the past, Georgina thought, but she'd been intrigued about her roots; those who know little and are curious often are. She'd believed her maternal grandfather had died in the Second World War, and his father in the First World War, but it was hard to get any useful information when one's family was reticent. She had a longing to know - to meet the ghosts of the past and ask them what they thought.

"Somewhere in Germany or France, I think. Maybe. Nana didn't like to talk about it, you know that," Mrs Crawford told her, wondering what had brought this up. "How is the new job? Still liking it?"

"The job is fine. The people are nice, but the place is a bit weird. Creepy. He was wounded wasn't he – and taken to that hospital somewhere? Nana said he never came home but no one really knew." Georgina couldn't get the hospital out of her mind. Her parents had asked why she wanted to give up a job in a busy, large and well-equipped hospital to work at some rundown country unit far from home. Georgina hadn't been able to quite put her finger on why but had told herself the working hours were better, she didn't have to commute so far if she stayed with her friend, and besides the place had called to her. Odd though that sounded. It was the right thing to do. Something had stirred but they would not understand such thoughts or reasoning.

"Blossom Rise, I think, or some name to do with flowers. Nana said he died of his wounds, but Auntie Marie reckons he ran off with someone. There was a rumour he'd taken up with some nurse, but I was only little, and I don't remember it very well. Apparently, someone from the hospital he'd been at came – A Mr Cameron or some name like that. Marie remembered it as she couldn't stop staring, said the chap was missing an arm and his face looked like had been burned half off. Marie was the eldest – she sat with Nana when this man arrived and gave him tea. Me and Joanne peeked in from the doorway, but we couldn't hear or understand everything that was said.

"It was late autumn – I do remember that as the trees were covered in red and gold. This Mr Cameron brought a letter from Leo, your Grandpa – said he'd left it at the hospital – but never had a chance to send it, he'd been brave in the place they'd been but would not talk about it to us. Grandpa had saved this man, pulled him out of danger and been wounded for it. He wouldn't speak much of it, either. Marie asked if she could write to him, as he was a link to her father. Cameron said no, he would not be contactable, as he wasn't sure where he was going, or how long for. Marie said his face, what was left of it was empty, as though a piece of his soul was missing. But she was fanciful that way."

"He wasn't an officer, just a soldier? After all, it's not usually another patient or a random soldier who comes with that kind of news, is it?" Georgina said, her mind awhirl.

Mrs Crawford sighed, "My memory isn't what it used to be. And I am basing a lot of what I know on what Marie said. This fellow Cameron said Grandpa had taken up with a nurse, and Nana had a right to know as it wasn't fair to live a lie. He wouldn't be coming home. Mother cried, and then Marie shooed me and my sister off to bed. I dreamt of that stranger for years, he haunted my dreams. This faceless, maimed man who'd come to take away my father. Dad was a ghost – I'd talk to him, ask him why he left. Tell him about things. Marie and your Nana thought I'd gone potty, but I needed him. I don't think I was sure, not even then."

"This maimed man – who could he have been?" Georgina asked. "Perhaps a soldier from his regiment? We've looked online to find the answer – but it was inconclusive. 'Missing in Action', or 'incomplete records' are all I got when I tried."

"James or John Cameron – that's all I remember – apart from his terrible injuries. Maybe it was because of his disability, his strange face, but the image of him stuck with me. Marie said it too. She'd wondered what had happened to him after the war – did he go home? Mother, your Nana, said Daddy had been killed and Marie agreed, at least then. It was much later when we were adults Marie said about the other woman, it was just a flippant comment after an argument we'd had when I left Peter. I don't remember the details –it was years ago. Maybe his death was a lie – to cover up the shame. Nana was proud, she'd never have admitted her husband had run off with some nurse. But you know what Auntie Marie was like – always had to be the centre of attention and the family drama queen. She was outraged when I divorced your father."

Georgina replied, "Yes she was, but it would be nice to know. He'd be long dead now, but it's possible there'd be another family?"

Her mother paused, she had assumed for a long time that her father had died, but there was no grave, no place to mourn. "We never knew, not for sure. I remember Marie telling me there had been an air-strike and Daddy was gone. Now I think about it I do remember some gossip about a 'fancy woman' but I thought it was idle chit-chat, that nastiness you sometimes get. I was young, only eight when I was told he'd died. There were several other fatherless families in the neighbourhood so at least we weren't alone in that way.

Divorce was a shameful thing then, and Mother was very proud. Fortunately, times have changed.

"I'd like to know for sure," Mrs Crawford decided. It's been over seventy years of not knowing, of believing something which might be wrong. I might have half-siblings if he really did run off. And there was never confirmation he'd been killed. Not officially – just this mutilated man who turned up, like a ghost he was – a shell of a man. I was too young to understand, of course."

"It must have been hard for you all," Georgina said, knowing it had been. "Is it possible Grandpa ran off with someone?"

Her mother replied, "It's possible. Nana was not the easiest person to live with and they had been having difficulties before he went to war. She was very devout, but he wasn't and didn't want any more kids to bring up. Times were hard, women didn't work like they do now. All I know is my daddy went to war and didn't come home."

There was silence – the hurt and confusion from a woman who remembered growing up without a father, as many others had, and the awkwardness of a younger woman who'd never known such loss, or hardship.

"The new job – the Crater Hospital used to be called Blossom Rise Hospital. Arabella reckons it was a hospital in the war. Bit of a coincidence," Georgina said, thoughtfully. "There's a huge bomb crater just behind this weird old bunker. It's out of bounds - health and safety. I don't know why it isn't pulled down, to be honest. But if a bomb had missed the buildings but landed close by wouldn't it still have caused damage? Perhaps Grandpa was there? I can see what I can find out. It's...it's haunted, so they say."

Mrs Crawford replied, "Nana refused to talk about it much, but there *was* a letter from Blossom Rise or Hill, I suppose it might have been. Marie found amongst her papers when she was clearing Nana's house. It was scrunched up like someone had made a ball of it, but your Nana had kept it. I didn't read it, but Marie did. I just knew he never came home. I didn't have a Dad.. Maybe he had a fancy woman - who knows. There were so many secrets, family lies I suppose.

"What does it matter now? It was a long time ago, and I'd like to talk about something else, darling."

The conversation turned to more mundane topics – the neighbour's new puppy, the price of milk at the supermarket, and the latest soap opera. Yet Georgina's mind was only half on the conversation. What was in that bunker? Who was this man who'd visited? What secrets lay in that place?

October 1943

The thirtieth consecutive day of rain pelted onto paving which had seen better days two decades ago and was now a patchwork of cracks, half-hearted repairs and, here and there, slippery boards. There was a war on, and money for repairs was scarce. The sky was iron-grey and desolate, as though rain was all there was, and the sun was a mere legend. Many believedthis was true, or at least grumbled as much. The sky had always held Mother Nature's power; more recently it held death on screaming wings made by the hand of man.

Figures hurried by beneath sodden umbrellas, if they were lucky, and ran for cover if they were not. A uniformed man limped as briskly as he could manage, one hand clutched a walking cane, the other wrapped around a large umbrella. Beside him strode a smaller, female figure, also in uniform, and sheltering beneath the arms of the umbrella. They were close but trying to appear not to be.

"Will this ever end? It seems like there is nothing but rain, rain and war," the smaller figure said, turning her face to his, and searching, for answers no one knew.

"The war must end, one way or the other, Mabel. The world cannot endure this unrelenting horror forever. We will win this awful conflict or be destroyed. As for the rain – it will end, and the sun will rise," her companion said, but the eyes which stared at the sky were not filled with hope. The man was in his mid-thirties, but his haggard face looked ten years older, such was the burden of loss he carried, and the responsibility for other men's lives. War aged a man. The woman looked younger and had once been wide-eyed and

innocent, but the world had seen that innocence stripped
away, like skin beneath a knife.

He pulled her close, glancing around in case any
onlookers should see them, but everyone was preoccupied
with staying dry and their own business. "The world has gone
mad, and politics with it, but we have each other. Even in the
rain, you are beautiful."

The woman held herself in his embrace for just a
moment, then pulled away, "Not here, Leo. We must keep it
professional."

Reluctantly he nodded and said louder, "I am healing well
enough. The doctor tells me the limp will be permanent and
I'll never be strong again, but I'll keep my leg and live to fight
another day. Men like me are needed, and there are few
enough of us these days. I can serve my country in other
ways."

`With that, he looked at something distant – perhaps a
foreign land. "Living another day is all we have these awful
times. Each one is precious, for tomorrow the Nazis may be at
our door. And I can't say I am keen to return to the field of
war."

He touched her arm, "I love you, Mabel, for what love in
war is worth. Now be a good girl and fetch my case. I'll meet
you inside, we are early anyway." He handed her the umbrella
and hiding in the shelter of the doorway lit a cigarette and
looked out towards the wards filled with the damaged, the
insane and the dying. Ghosts of men, some said, and it was
true. Leo felt hollow, incomplete. Something other than blood
and flesh had been lost in that foreign theatre of war. In the
horror he'd asked God to help him, to stop this awful mess,
but all he'd heard was the scream of his comrades, the
thunder of bombs and silence from the Man Upstairs. Once a
Catholic – he'd cursed God's holy name when another of his
men tumbled lifelessly beside him. How could a loving God
allow such slaughter? Leo knew his faith was gone, shot away
piece by piece, and his soul with it.

Thinking of all the friends he'd lost, all the wickedness of
man, made real in a war that had shaken the world to its iron
core, the man called Leo limped towards the bunker door, his

second home now his wounds were healing. Strategy was needed, and Leo had been behind the lines, laying mines and infiltrating where he could. He was, so he'd learned, one of the last survivors of his unit.

"She'll be the death of me if those bombs don't get us first." He glanced back towards where she'd gone. "But I'd gladly die if it was in her arms."

Mabel was the only thing of beauty he'd seen in far too long. Too many years living on the edge of a knife, where fear was one's constant companion and loss one's daily brethren, changed a person, and not for the better. Especially a man like Leo Campbell, who could not admit to his fear, was honoured for his perseverance and bravery under fire, and his cunning.

It was all a sham. All of it – civilisation, decency, morality– had been tested, and found wanting. His own father had been killed in Ypres and his mother was forced to raise five children on a widow's pension. He'd gained extra money and food poaching – knew how to use a gun. Eyes closed, he saw his mother's face as he went to war – the fear, the regrets, and the sadness. Such emotions mirrored in his wife's younger face.

"It's my duty," he'd said. "We cannot let the likes of Herr Hitler control Europe. It will be over soon enough." He'd believed that then.

Leo laughed. But there was no mirth. Four long and terrifying years of war had proven Hitler was not a man who would give up his wicked machinations easily, and Britain would stand against him, alone if she had to. Neither side would capitulate until the enemy was in the streets and at the door.

The world had gone mad with slaughter in the War to End All Wars a generation past – but that had been a lie as well. Politics, death and lies entwined as the casualties grew. Freedom exacted a terrible price. Leo knew that as the bodies had piled up around him in that small French town – now little more than a shell. He'd led what was left of his men into battle, when their captain had been slain and pushed back the enemy, gaining some useful intelligence for his pains. But it had all been futile when the next regiment of panzers rolled in, and he and his men found the landmines as they'd tried to retreat. The blood still flowed when he closed his eyes.

Leo dreamt of the faces of the men he'd shot or bayonetted behind the fluctuating German lines. Men like him. Simple men who had been sent to war or signed up unknowing of the horror. Politicians made war, but soldiers died in it far removed from the seat of their government. In this war, civilians lived in fear of the blitz from the sky. Even the clouds were not safe in a world of madness and blood. Was this the end of days? The final judgement for Man's sins? Leo did not know, and his faith in a good divinity had bled away on the fields of war.

He longed to be far away, on a picnic blanket in the Cotswolds with Mabel. Home with his wife, Audrey, and his daughters, his conscience said. He'd lost much of that conscience in this war. What was adultery, when man sinned the ultimate sin for his country, for freedom, every single day?

Ostensibly Blossom Rise had been a private sanatorium for those sons of the wealthy who needed tending in a small country hospital, and then when Europe had been ripped by war it had become half a dozen wards used to treat those who had returned from the Great War broken or insane. After the Great War, the unit had fallen into disrepair – forgotten or ignored like so many of the unfortunate soldiers who'd passed through but left still clinging on to half a life. There had been a few in-patients – usually those persons whose families wished for them to be out of sight and mind, but not neglected. It was full of ghosts, so some whispered. And he knew the nurses gossiped. Once he'd have dismissed such talk as nonsense, irreligious and foolish, but he'd seen men he'd known to be dead walk the wards. Men from his dreams.

His friend James Cameron, half his face burned away, and one arm nothing but a stump had succumbed to death after a heroic but futile struggle.

Leo had seen James only last night limping the ward in the half-light – a shell of a man ravaged and hollow. But stalking like he'd once done – searching and alert.

A nurse had tried to usher the bandaged form back to his bed, but James had vanished when she returned with his medication. Disappeared. In some ways it had been a mercy that James had gone, his friend had been so badly wounded and what life would he have – no face, one arm, partly crippled and more than half-mad? He had not wanted to live like that – a burden for his mother. Later Leo asked himself if James had been been at the hospital or was lying burned and maimed in that awful town. Was he just a memory, a guilty horror?

They'd talked, or at least Leo thought they'd had, in the small hours of the morning when the pain was too much to sleep, and the morphine hadn't clouded their minds. But it was all so vague, so confused. Reality turned on its head in war, and time in this hospital – fluctuating between pain, medication and sleep was strange.

He'd told James about his family, his wife, and James had spoken of a sweetheart, and a mother raising children alone. He too had lost his father in the Great War, and his mother's heart had broken when he went to war. Each promised to visit the other's family if only one survived. James had told Leo to seek the happiness he'd earned. If he didn't love his wife, then staying for duty was worse than not staying at all. Both men knew what duty meant, and what horror and sadness it could bring. Sometimes it was best to let go.

"That nurse is in love with you, mate. She doesn't sit next to my bed after her shift is over. She doesn't spend her ration tokens on the likes of me. Not that anyone would likely want to look at this face now." His voice was little more than a weak croak, and Leo realised then James knew he wouldn't make it.

The two had arrived together, or so Leo thought – one burned, one broken. Both were little more than ghosts when they arrived. Mabel had been surprised James had lasted as long as he had, and every day of life for Leo was precious. It had been her tender care that meant he'd keep his leg. "But I made a promise to Audrey. What about my children?" Leo had whispered in the darkness to his friend when the nurses were occupied elsewhere.

James turned towards him painfully. "Have you not realised life is too short to settle for second best? It's for living. Mabel understands you, Audrey doesn't. Even if we live, we aren't the same men we were. We are broken, we are ghosts. The men who went to war are gone, my friend. Take the life you can, the love you can and don't let go. You've been through too much to live a lie."

That much speaking had tired the wounded and dying man and he lapsed back into the semi-torpid state he so often inhabited since they'd arrived several weeks ago. Leo wondered if James had given up. He couldn't blame him if he had. Leo had prayed for death, as well as life, more than once – but had been left in this halfway house between one and the other. He'd prayed in the burning darkness – and silence had been his answer.

Leo thought he remembered pulling his friend away, blood gushing from what was left of James's arm and the stench of burning flesh, he'd bound the arm before James bled to death and then carried him, staggering towards the cover of a building. The pain from his own injuries a perfidious master, and then the blood-red darkness had come. It was all so strange, so awful. Real and unreal.

James had somehow stood by his bed when the fever took Leo and grasped his hand, "Remember what I said. Take what you can, when you can. Do not live a lie. I am going soon, but I'll not forget you and I owe you this service. Be with the one you love, forever." James had been there every time Leo had awoken, but no one else had seen him when Leo mumbled his friend's name in his delirium.

Leo had seen the fear in the nurse's face when he'd mentioned seeing James, and she knew the bed next to Leo's was empty and had been for more than a week, but his fever had returned and time ebbed and flowed in this half-life he lived. Souls did not rest easy when taken too soon.

"Am I mad?" Leo had asked. "It's the morphine," Sister Duggan told him, smartly. But he noticed she'd crossed herself. "Father Whitaker will be round later. I know you've lapsed but it might do you good." She meant it in kindness, but it was far too late for Leo to find comfort there. Leo had accepted it. After all, morphine could play strange games, and he'd been halfway to heaven when he'd come here, or more likely halfway to hell – of that he was certain.

Nurses gossiped, and when he'd seen the apparition again the following night after he'd rallied, he'd whispered to the nurse on duty. "James is dead. Poor bugger. He knew it and so did I. But he was here, I saw him, I spoke to him."

"It's the drugs," she said, but didn't sound confident and stared at the empty bed. "It must be. Go back to sleep."

"But I saw him, and so did you. Sister said it's the drugs, and so do you but I am not convinced. I heard you talking to that other nurse. Leo's eyes darted to the empty bed. "Or has my mind been ripped apart as well?"

Nurse Emma had hesitated. This man needed to know such truth as there was in a world of lies, blood and fear. "You aren't mad, Leo. Not unless I am too, and Sister Duggan, and Lieutenant Ellis. We've all seen these shadows. War and pain do strange things to people, but I think it's more. Souls trapped where they died. This place served in the Great War and probably before, as it does now, and some of the other girls have seen nurses long dead in the corridors, or men with old uniforms. I've worked in other places and seen similar there. They won't harm you, they are just sad and lost – that's all. Rest and soon you'll be able to leave us. James muttered something about a letter, but he was delirious at the end." She fussed over Leo, and then whispered, "Don't tell Sister Duggan I've talked to you about it. She'll have me scrubbing bedpans for a week."

"Can you help me with a letter, Nurse Emma? Don't mention it to Mabel yet though, I want to talk to her," Leo asked, as Nurse Wagstaff brought him tea, and checked on him. She knew he'd taken James' death hard and was concerned for him. She'd been told he was brave, yet she saw sadness and despair on his face. She saw the war, and the toll it exacted from flesh and spirit. But she'd seen his eyes follow Mabel Horton and seen her sat at his bedside after-hours reading and watching. There was a spark there, a spark of life and something more. Togetherness. It was hard not to form an attachment to these poor wounded boys, but all the medical staff had seen enough come in a stretcher, or the back of a wagon and patched up what was left. Some left to return home, some left in a box. Far too many.

"Tomorrow. I can help you tomorrow. And I'll keep your secrets," Nurse Emma Wagstaff told him, a sly grin at intrigue crossing her face. "I've seen the way you look at her."

* * *

Leo sighed, returning to the present, and his personal ghosts of memory. He missed his friend and had kept silent that he'd seen him again since James had died. The letter he'd written to his wife had disappeared and he'd assumed the nurse had taken it away. But memory played strange, disturbing games and Leo was no longer sure what was real and what was not. All he knew for certain was war and his love for Mabel. Everything else was a fever-dream or a lie. Or possibly not. These days nothing was normal, nothing was as it had been. He felt like a ghost watching a world it cannot touch but used to belong in. Leo knew he'd left more than blood and flesh in France. Some wounds would kill a man, some would make him less than he was, and some would linger, perfidious and unseen.

His recovery had been slow, and the injuries he'd taken in the blast would likely be life-long. He could not even remember the journey to the field hospital in France. The journey back to England was a memory etched in pain and sorrow, and he remained in pain, fire, blood and death. But since he'd been at Blossom Rise, he'd learned every day of life was precious, not to mention precarious.

Mabel expected nothing from him, unlike his demanding wife at home. And she understood, as only someone who had seen the face of war could. Although his memory was patchy, Leo remembered, vivid as the day, when a brown-haired nurse, with eyes like jade, had smiled at him. Leo had suddenly found the will to live in that smile.

Of all the men she'd nursed, and some she'd lost, he was the one who'd touched her heart the most. At once so strong, and so frail. Such a warrior, and such a boy. She'd held his hand when he'd cried for his mother and his friend in his fear and fever, and she'd tended to him long after her shift was over There had never been pity, just kindness and compassion.

After she'd seen him and James the evening they had arrived, Mabel had cried, secretly. There were never tears in front of 'her boys'. Four long years of war and patching up what remained–be it body, mind or soul – took its toll. Mabel's mother had wept when she had left to 'do her bit'. But Mabel's duty was clear. Mabel owed it to the brothers she'd lost, and her father who had returned from the Great War a different man, halfway to becoming a ghost. These wounded soldiers needed compassion, understanding and a non-judgemental shoulder on which to cry. Mabel had seen what war could do to even the strongest of men. She could not risk her life as her menfolk had done – but she could dedicate it to helping what was left after they returned.

Before the war Leo would have been shocked to consider adultery, even bigamy; Mabel had reminded Leo that life was worth living, there was hope in darkness, and compassion in the depths of war. And James had told him to live it. She'd even listened to his crazy thoughts about James Cameron's ghost with sympathy and understanding. She had seen the shapes of people who had died of their wounds around the hospital. She'd even told him of the Secret Ledger – a document filled with sightings, bizarre happenings and the accounts of men whose bodies had left the world and yet didn't know it. Such a wise head, and eyes that showed Leo he was not mad, not yet.

"Emma has seen the book, and so have I. Sister thinks it's hidden but we all know about it. It's in the bunker, locked away. You've sat beside it when you've helped with their planning on your better days. A man like you has information, and Britain needs all the help she can get. I know you do that with some of the others here."

Leo had tried to protest, but he couldn't lie to Mabel. And a number of the officers had been 'briefed' when they were well enough. Every tool, every tidbit of the enemy's positions and armaments helped.

"Sister threatened to burn it, but Doctor Jones won't have it. He thinks it's valuable – medical information. He's keen on psychiatry you know. He won't profess to have seen anything himself, but we all think he has. Sister is a Catholic – she says the only ghost is the Holy Ghost – but she protests too loudly if you ask me. This place is full of ghosts – and some of them are still living."

* * *

Leo stopped, as the rain spattered around them both. "I'm not going back to Audrey, my wife. I don't think I've loved her for a long time. She is just focused on the children – she'll not be able to care for me, as you do. I'll be a burden and she will make sure I know it. She doesn't understand. It sounds stupid when I say it aloud, but the war has changed me. The man Audrey married is gone. When this madness is over will you be my wife, Mabel? I will divorce Audrey, although she'll not be happy, I've told her. We've lived a lie long enough. We need to take hope and happiness where we can. Too many lives have been destroyed. Why fight for freedom, then live in chains?"

Mabel stared at Leo, "You'd leave your family for me? But isn't she Catholic? – There could be no divorce."

"Yes, she is. I was a Catholic, but not very devout, now I am not anything but a cynic. We can go far away, the coast or the Cotswolds, live as man and wife. Who'd know but us? War changes everything and morality is on its head. Besides she may have found another to warm her bed." Leo did not look convinced. "I need you, Mabel, I can't face the world alone. I have my ghosts, and you understand that. Audrey wouldn't – she'd mock me. She can't stand weak men, and I can't go back to my old job like this. This war has to end for us, one way or the other. We can be happy. Surely we both deserve that?"

He was a ghost – alive – but still a shadeof who he'd been. Leo gazed into the distance – the man he'd been was long gone, dead and buried in mud, rubble and blood. As Mabel returned with his bag Leo limped into the bunker and knew his plans would make ghosts of other men before the war's end. But now he had something to cling on to. He'd not give up, and not give her up.

As he kissed her, they heard the screech of aircraft, then the darkness came again.

October 2015

It was gone 11 pm when Arabella and Georgina crept towards the door of the bunker. The security guard had passed that way ten minutes previously and was not due for another fifty minutes. Georgina hoped they could be in and out with answers by then.

"I am not even going to ask where you got the key from...I hope you know what you are getting us into. This place is a death-trap, even I can tell that. The back wall is half held up with rotten bricks and broken timber and there's no electricity. It's ruddy cold too," Arabella grumbled, afraid she'd regret helping her friend. "You owe me a whole crate of wine, I hope you know this."

"Yes, yes. Now keep it down, that guard has sharp ears, apparently. I checked the camera doesn't work here. Although that isn't common knowledge – apparently it gets fixed every so often and breaks again." Georgina pulled a torch from her bag and waggled the key into a rusty lock. "I hope this works."

"So do I, I might get some peace from your nagging..." Arabella muttered.

Water dripped from the ceiling, at least they hoped it was water. The torch illuminated a sliver of the rickety staircase leading downwards into a cloying and fetid dark. "I hope this isn't a joke, because it's not funny," said Arabella cautiously.

"You can wait here. By yourself. If you like..." Georgina snapped, although she'd been thinking much the same.

"I'll take my chances with the person holding the torch, thanks. Besides, it's the solos who always get eaten by the nasty monster."

Arabella felt a poke in the ribs, then a hand slipped into her own. "You aren't helping. Come on, Nurse, don't tell me you are afraid of ghosts."

She squeezed Georgina's hand, "No, but I am afraid of ending up as a broken heap at the bottom of this stairway."

They moved downwards, slow, minding every slippery step. The darkness expanded into a dim room large enough to hold a table, a dozen chairs, a large map of Europe and a radio set. Lights flickered, at a desk in the corner a large, thick and dusty book rested.

Blossom Rise Hospital and Sanatorium it pronounced, title written in now-brownish ink on a ragged silken cover.

As Georgina squinted in the dim light Arabella whispered, "Why are the lights on? I thought there was no power?"

Georgina stared at her, then looked around the room, "Maybe it's intermittent. Here – it's too gloomy to read much, hold the torch. We've not got long."

Arabella took the torch with some reluctance and tried to look at the map. "Hey, that's Europe in wartime – look there are little swastikas on most of it. Shit."

It had taken a lot of persuasion and bribery for her to learn the whereabouts of the Secret Ledger. And even more persuasion to enlist Arabella in the hunt for answers. "My grandpa was here. I am sure of it. And he disappeared – Nana said he died, but my aunt reckoned he ran off with another woman. And there was this man, Mr Cameron or something. Had all his face burned off and one arm missing, he'd brought a letter from Grandpa. My Nana never really got over it, and Mum didn't either. Whether he left or died it doesn't much matter – he left his family alone either way. Maybe he'd been a coward and that was the shameful family secret, or maybe he was a hero. I have to know."

"I can understand that. Maybe there is a simple answer. Maybe he died, I bet most of the poor sods who came here did." Arabella eyed the great, old book and the table.

It was damp, musty and Arabella felt a cold draught. Shivering she saw a sliver of darkness through a crack in the wall. She shifted, and her shoes crunched on something.

Georgina was focused on the book and Arabella dared not look down.

A huge tome, smelling of old books, age and musty cupboards, it was indeed a relic of the past. It had been burned around the edges and by the light of the torch, she peered at it. "What secrets are you hiding?" Georgina whispered.

She read page after page of spidery, faded writing. "This is a book of ghosts. My god, how many people died or were wounded in war after war?" She leafed through until she found around the middle of the book the records she sought.

"15th August 1943 – Pte James Cameron, Kings IVth died of wounds sustained in Dieppe. Leaves mother and two sisters. Brother deceased. Father deceased.

17th August 1943 – Cpl Henry Percival – returned to active duty.

15th September 1943 – Air raid. Blossom Farm hit, 6 cows, 1 person killed.

30th September 1943 – Air raid. 15 fatalities in Dewry St, 5 wounded brought to BR. Nurse Green among fatalities.

3rd October 1943 – Nurse Mabel Horton, wounded in air raid. Brothers deceased.

3rd October 1943 – Nurse Emma Wagstaff, wounded in air raid, later died of wounds

3rd October 1943 – Captain Peter James – Kings IXth – reconnaissance – injured in air-raid.

3rd October 1943 – Lt Leo Campbell, Kings IVth hit in air-raid. Leaves widow and five children and mother; father deceased. Awarded gallantry medal Dieppe 1942, posthumously awarded bar for pulling Nurse Horton, Nurse Wagstaff and Captain James from the rubble. Died of his wounds 5th October 1943.

5th October 1943 – Bunker decommissioned – as unsafe.

10th October 1943 – Nurse Watkins reports seeing Lt Campbell walking the grounds.

31st October 1943 – Doctor Carridine, Dr Renfew and Sister Duggan report seeing Campbell and Cameron in conversation.

1st November 1943 – Sister Duggan resigns, Dr Renfew resigns."

"There's a few more resignations and reports of strange goings-on. People seeing a limping man or a woman crying. The next entry is 1973 – I think that's when the place was reopened. At least A Wing," Georgina said, her voice trembling slightly.

Arabella guided the torch down. "I didn't want to say but I think we are standing on someone....Horton? That's not a particularly common name – could be a relative of our Dr Horton?"

Bones and scraps of fabric lay beneath the desk, although it was impossible to tell how long they'd been there or to whom they had belonged. "Keep reading, Georgie..."

"3rd October 1973 - Nurse Wilson reports seeing limping man in old wing.

3rd October 1975 – Dr Carridine reports sounds of screaming and sight of nurse in military uniform."

"That can't be the same Carridine, surely?" Arabella said, wide-eyed.

5th October 1977 - Nurse in military uniform seen in ward 8. Man in uniform seen crossing the path towards her.

15th August 2000 – one-armed and disfigured man filmed crossing towards the bunker.

3rd October 2000 – Man with walking cane heard screaming a name – Mabel."

She flicked through more pages, "It goes on – look. Every year or couple of years there's someone who reports seeing or hearing a man or woman in uniform, crying or walking the grounds. And who completes this book? There are references as far back as 1910 to ghostly goings-on and as recent as last year. There are newspaper cuttings, a bit faded and mucky now but still."

What's the date?" Georgina shivered. "Leo Campbell must have been Grandpa, so he saved those people, those nurses from the raid. He was a hero. Maybe he was in love with one of the women he rescued. I wonder if she lived?" As she turned to take the torch from her friend a light on the wall brightened. And a siren blared, the sound of doom itself. In fear, Arabella fumbled with the torch as she was handing it over and it bounced away.

"Air Raid! Take Cover!" The voice bellowed from the air, and like dust dancing a man, walking cane in his hand, dived past, and through the astonished women towards a small, pretty nurse, whose face was lined with fear. She had not been there a moment before. She turned, unseeing the living women and breathed, 'Leo, save yourself' before falling to the ground beneath a shower of debris and fire.

Blood oozed around their feet; Arabella and Georgina were frozen to the spot as bricks fell around them, and dust choked the nose and throat.

They watched, unable to turn aside as the chaos rained its deadly force around them, and walls tumbled. The ghostly man, his uniform bloodied staggered up, and scrambled through spectral stones, and burning wood. His hands tugged at bricks, at beams and he seemed to ignore the crimson circle widening on his chest and the fire licking over his back. "Mabel! I'm here, darling. I'll find you." The sound hung like the last notes of a song, oddly distinct from the echoing crashes.

As the lights dimmed, they saw him haul up a still form and rush past them and up the stairs before returning.

"Shit. Let's go." Arabella was shaking. "It's real. Or it was. There *are* ghosts here!"

The torch had winked out and the two nurses stumbled up the stairs in the dark, not caring about safety and dived through the door into the rain and a dark, dark night. They were covered in dust, and mortar, "My shoes are wet and I'm too scared to look in case it isn't rain," Georgina squeaked and running, they hared across a path which had seen better days seven decades and more, ago. "My mother will think I've flipped if I tell her."

As the door to the bunker closed behind them the ledger, which had remained unscathed in all the mayhem, closed on the newest entry. Then the darkness came.

War and Beyond

Marta Moran Bishop

Prologue

Funny how your dreams are a gateway into your subconscious that can heal old wounds and bring back memories. Not that the memories of only a year ago or the details aren't still vivid enough without dreaming them too. But the color and terror dim with time, though I believe they stay in your bones long after if not forever. I thought sitting on the edge of my bed shaking with horror and drenched in sweat from the dreams.

I'm glad I chose to sleep upstairs last night, at least I didn't wake the children. I've held each of them after one of their own terrible dreams. We all have them and today I will begin writing them down. Perhaps, much like Anne Franke's Journal at least for a time they will remind and teach others in the future when the world begins to heal, and history will not repeat itself again.

My name is Melinda Bishop, though most know me as Mel. But who is Mel but a made-up character I created to survive what I knew in my bones something was coming.

It wasn't safe to be a woman living alone and for sure not an old woman. But I'm thin enough, my hair is short enough, that with it pulled back, a cap on my head, loose jeans, and clothes I've passed for a man and kept myself and the children safe. I've learned to be nearly invisible and rarely noticed my most, though at times I feel as if I've lost a part of who I am.

Chapter One

That fateful day as I sat in the doctor's office waiting my turn, the boom of the low flying planes knocked out the windows, sprinkling glass everywhere and followed by blasts as bombs hit the taller buildings in the distance. Smoke rose like a cloud of dust covered the once blue sky, shutting out the sun.

People screamed and chairs tipped over as they ran for the door or fell to the floor to seek cover. The area of this office was a way off from ground zero, but who knew if we would be ground zero soon. As I crawled out of the office, taking the stairs instead of the elevator, the building shook again with a blast as another bomb hit something else.

So many people screaming, some running, some huddled together, many of the old who couldn't walk quickly were left behind, while others were helped by family members, friends, or even strangers. It wasn't that I didn't want to help them, but something told me I needed to get out of there, others needed me more.

Through the smoke, I saw my old truck, parked right near the entrance to the street, ready for flight so to speak. I've always had a bit of prescience, which is both a blessing and a curse. Today it was a blessing.

Unfortunately, I would need to drive nearer to where I believed the bombs had hit in order to get home. Way too near for my taste, perhaps even through some of it. That's something I'd find out as I drove, with luck I'd make it home.

Fate is an odd thing, and it was fate that found me driving towards ground zero, not away from it, for it was there that I saw the carnage. The dead and dying lying on the street, homes and buildings demolished, and filthy, blood-covered Margarita and Tony standing next to an African American man and a Hispanic woman lying amidst the rubble of an ice cream shop, April and Andy just a few feet away. As I stopped and pulled over to the curb, Tony ran up to me, begging for help, as Margarita crouched on the ground next to April and Andy.

"Please help us,' Margarita cried out. 'Their parents begged us to get April and Andy out of here and save them. We have nowhere to go, both of us lost our house when the bomb hit in the first wave."

"We'll put the young ones in the truck first and cover them with the old tarp I have in the compartment behind the seat. You two can ride up here with me. I believe my house will be safe, at least safer than it is here in the city." I said quietly.

After carefully placing the two youngest in the back of the truck, covering them completely with the tarp, the older boy and girl got into the front seat and I was behind the wheel. Backing out a way to get clear from some of the rubble, we inched our way out of the area and made it through the war-torn area, through the streets, past police and ambulance sirens, and onto the highway. Not one of us spoke until we were well away from the city.

Both of the older two were sobbing, holding each other as the tears streaked through the dirt and blood running down their faces. "We'll check for injuries when we are at the house. There is no time right now and no way of knowing if another bomb will hit, or if some will start shooting. I'm sure the hospitals are overwhelmed, and I don't believe any of you are badly hurt. At least I hope not."

Their brown eyes looked at me, not saying a word, just a nod. Yet the farther away we drove I could tell that they were beginning to fear that maybe I was a danger to them too. In a way that wasn't surprising, I was a stranger, and all their lives they had been told to stay away from strangers and to make it worse, I was an old white stranger too.

"My name is Melinda, but you can call me Mel, most do."

Out of the corner of my eye, I watched them eye me up and down until curiosity got the better of them both.

"Yes, I am an old woman, not a man, but I found it safer if people thought I was an old man. Being an old woman alone hasn't been very safe for a while."

"I'm Margarita and this is Tony, we are friends, though our parents didn't much like it because we aren't of the same race.' Margarita said, beginning to cry again. 'I suppose what they thought doesn't matter anymore does it?"

"Well, I don't care what your race or heritage is, if you won't care I'm an old white woman pretending to be a man. Do you think that will work for us all? You can call me Mel, though April and Andy may want to call me Mimi till they are older."

Glancing out the back window Tony asked. "Can we pull over? The young ones in the back are stirring and I don't think they should wake up alone."

Pulling onto the side of the highway I replied. "You are right Tony. Would you two prefer to put them on your laps up here, or go back and get under the tarp with them in the back?"

"I think we'd all feel safer up here together." He replied as Margarita and he got out of the truck, and carefully picked up the young ones, and carried them into the cab of the truck.

"Where are we going?" Margarita asked, holding the young girl on her lap.

"I have a house quite a way out from the city. It is on a lonely street. I live there with my horse, mule, some chickens, two cats, and a dog. It might be safe, or safer than most places will be. But I think we will still need to be careful for a long while who knows how far this war will spread or when it will end. But first, we will need to stop and get you all some clothing. Warmer coats, boots, shoes, jeans, T-shirts, underwear, jammies, and other things you will need."

Chapter Two

As we drove on, and couldn't hear the bombing any longer, April and Andy woke up.

"Who are you? Where are we? Where are our parents?" Andy asked, April crying and clinging to her almost new brother.

"Hi little ones, you can call me Mimi if you want. We will talk about your parents later. But for now, what do you all think about living on a farm for a while?"

"What kind of a farm?" Andy asked shyly.

"It's a small farm, with fruit trees, a garden, a horse, mule, chickens, and blueberry bushes. A dog named Buster, and the cats Gabe and Axel. We'd all have our chores to do each day. But those chores would grow as you learned and grew older. What do you think?"

"I love cats, April chimed in." Her dirty little face looked at me with a bit of hope.

"Can I ride the horse?" Andy asked.

"Yes, you can all ride Dink and Ruth, as you get to know them and learn to ride," I answered.

Both children appeared to have blocked out the memories of their parents and past lives (at least for now.)

A smile lit the faces of all four children. It was the first I'd seen from them. *Oh, I know as time goes by, we will all have to face the past. But not today.*

"Mel, will we be safe at your house?" Tony inquired.

"I won't ever lie to any of you. But that is a question that I don't have an answer for. I believe we will be, the house is far enough away, and on a very quiet street. But we may have days we need to hide in the basement. Times we must make the house look unoccupied. I just don't know how far this war will extend or what the fall out from displaced people fleeing the cities will be."

"How can we appear as if no one lives in the house in the winter, won't the smoke from the furnace and the lights at night show?" Margarita asked quietly.

"I've made an apartment in the basement, I have electric heaters, so we may need to turn off the furnace at times, shut all the curtains, and learn to live with very little light at night."

"What about the outdoor animals?" Andy asked.

What a bright young boy he was. I thought.

"I did prepare an incase scenario, that I built over the years, but thought it was because of the possibility of climate change, not war. A part of that was building a stall in what used to be the garage and putting a chicken coup in there too. The Dink, Ruth, and Buster will need to be in there during any hours that are needed to keep us all safe. But on a lighter note, I do have music, a TV with movies we can watch. Games we can play and a lot of books we can read when we are huddled in the basement rooms."

That was the beginning of it all.

Chapter Three

I can hear the Dink and Ruth moving around in their makeshift stall in what used to be the garage under the house, it's a comforting sound, as is the sound of the sleeping children in our rooms in the basement, cuddled next to the dog, and cat. I built these rooms and the stalls before the world and the country headed toward internal war, and climate change had tipped over the line.

In the beginning, after my husband passed on and the world changed so much, I would sometimes forget my name, it had been so long since anyone used it. When the children were younger, they called me Mimi, though some have grown up enough to call me Mel, it is nice to hear my name again, even though Mel is only the part of my name that it was safe to use.

You see, when the war started, we lost the internet that so many depended upon for their communication and entertainment. When the internet went down, so did the property records, now they are all paper files, and I transferred the property to the name I made up Mel Bishop. It is not safe for a woman to own land these days, so it was easier for me to convert my name from Melinda to Mel. I am thin enough that when I do have to go out and about, I can change my appearance just enough, that no one notices that I'm an old woman and not an old man. People rarely notice old people anymore, and now there are fewer people than there once were.

My hair is completely white now, not a speck of brown, or gray left from my younger days before the pandemic hit the world. In a way the pandemic both made and broke people, there were those like me, that learned to live alone, to be alone, and to plan for those days that would mean life or death for us all in the future.

For some it made things worse, they clung harder to guns, and various religions. Gods of every type, leaving science behind, carrying their fear so high that they'd shoot first, and think later. Many claimed it was what the Christian Bible called 'The End Times,' and feared that nothing could stop it. I never did understand why they clung to their guns if they thought they were going to die anyway. But it was the way things were then, and probably in too many places still are. I can't tell you anything about that, having no access anymore to the internet, or news stations. We do have TVs and DVRs and many movies, old TV shows on tape, and of course books and games, to keep us occupied if we aren't sewing, cooking, weeding, or tending the animals.

I first met thirteen-year-old Margarita and fourteen-year-old Andy sleeping on the streets and brought them here. I asked them where their parents where they stood there looking at me with a hollow-eyed stare before they began crying. Dirt running down their faces as the tears fell, they told me they died in the bombings. I did try to find their family, but without records, and the world turned upside down it was impossible. I remember so well how each day for months on end, I'd go out and look for them, but to no avail. Margarita and Andy weren't related but had found each other in the madness that was. They hid from most people, and ate what they could find, when they could find it, a little black boy, and a Latina girl just wasn't wanted by the gun-toting city folks.

Of course, now that gasoline and ammunition are so scarce, there is less chance of mass shootings, and so many of the worst of them are gone, died off, or moved on to the more fertile pickings in the larger cities. Those of us who stayed in this area farm, raise animals, and barter for what we need, though we don't socialize much, at least not yet. Perhaps one day when the world settles down.

Chapter Four

We still use the upper part of the house most of the year, except when the marauders are in the area, or it is too hot up there, and the central air can only be run sporadically. Then we come down here, between the solar panels and the Tesla battery backup it produces enough to cook on the little electric stove, run the small heater, and in the summer it is cooler. No wisp of smoke escapes through the chimney to give any signs of life to the world, and with the Dink, and Ruth in the stall in what used to be the garage, no sign of life exists. We even built a small chicken coop in a corner of the garage, oh not enough to make the area uncomfortable for Dink and Ruth, but enough for us to get a few eggs.

We were virtually invisible unless someone walked behind the house and saw the garden, greenhouse, or fruit trees, the planting season has changed, and the greenhouse is only used in late winter, through early spring. Dink, and Ruth, play in the paddocks in the early morning, and after dusk sets in, except in the winter, the trees that line the street in front hide them from most people's view, though it has become less risky, it is rare for anyone to come down this street anymore.

Once, and only once did I have to use my guns to fend off those who tried to take over the house, but that was before I found the children. I told them about it, so they know why we must keep a lookout, but in all probability, it will not happen again, this street is difficult to find and nearly vacant, the closest house miles away. We are incredibly careful with the use of ammunition and gas, as it is so difficult to get now.

The few neighbors I had fled years ago, when the bombing got closer and closer to us and before Boston went under the ocean, and the coast forever changed. I was lucky to have found this land years ago, it is far enough inland, and high enough above sea level to not be impacted by that. Though, the winds and storms have gotten stronger each year. The winters are colder, and summers hotter.

Luckily, this street has always been off the beaten path, but feed for the animals would have been difficult without a lot of planning when things began to get worse.

I bought a bit extra every month of hay stretcher, grain, and hay, and filled both sheds to the top with hay, grain, and hay stretcher, plus I used one of the stalls in the barn for storage of chicken, canned goods, more hay, and grain. In the early days, we had to protect the animals against those that were hungry, frightened, and fleeing the bombed-out cities.

I hope Ray and Cassie are still in the area and will be able to grow hay again soon. But if not, I will find someone who can deliver. In the meantime, Margarita, Andy, and I have put up makeshift fencing around the field next to us, I think it is abandoned now. Last year we planted alfalfa, bluegrass, and clover, which helps to keep the need to use our stock of feed down.

It's so quiet now, we haven't heard any shelling in a few months, and summer is full-on now.

Yesterday I took my old trusty truck out for a short drive to see what the damage to the area was, find out what was still left, who was still left, and if I could buy a bit of gasoline for the generator anywhere.

So many of the homes and buildings are gone, and now the forest has taken over. But I did find a bit of gasoline. You can still see the graves of the dead.

All in all, at least we've been lucky so far.

As I sit here drinking the one cup of coffee, I allow myself a day and thinking, I heard Margarita and Andy get up and go to feed the animals, collect eggs for breakfast and let Dink and Ruth run a bit. I am so lucky to have them in my life, and when it is my time, they will inherit the house and land, along with April and Tony that is already written down in my will, though they don't know it yet.

Chapter Five

"Mimi, please tell us the story of how the world changed," April said plaintively.

"Yes, please Mimi." Tony chimed in.

I stopped gazing at the fake flames in the electric stove that warmed the room and looked at them. *What little darlings they both were, eight-year-old April with her black kinky hair, brown skin, and nine-year-old Tony with the look of what once had been called a Hispanic.*

"Come over here and sit by me," I said, watching them stand up and walk the few feet over to me, warming their backs against the fire. Their eager little eyes watched me with love. *Oh, how lucky I am to have them as company in my old age. It could have been different, I may never have run into their parents years ago, who begged me to save April and Tony as they lay dying in the ruins of their home.*

"Why don't you call Andy and Margarita down to hear the story too. Do you know where they are?"

"They both got up early, while it was still cool enough out to pick more vegetables and play with the horse and mule," April stated.

"We wanted to help them today, but we slept too late.' Tony replied soulfully. 'But they said we could help feed the animals when they bring them inside."

"It is true it will be getting sweltering hot in a few hours and Dink and Ruth will need to be brought in. At least they get to run outside for a bit at night and in the early morning. I expect it is difficult for them to be shut up in their basement stalls during the heat of the day. We will all need to go downstairs ourselves soon. Why don't we wait until it is hot, and I'll tell you all the story, and your mommas and papas can add what they know too."

"Okay, they both chimed in."

"I'll make your breakfast while you get washed up and dressed. After Margarita and Andy come back in, and we've had breakfast, I'll read to you before the sun goes down, it's hard to read by the one little lamp.

I'll tell you the story this evening, okay?"

"Yes, Mimi." They both chimed in.

Just then Margarita and Andy came bursting in the door.

"Mel, come see. The sunflowers are blooming again. Margarita yelled joyfully."

"How wonderful, let's all go see them. It will be a nice way to start the morning. We can have breakfast afterward."

Rushing out the door, past the chickens, stalls, and into the open, stopping for a moment to watch Dink and Ruth run and jump in the field, we climbed the berm and gazed at the field of sunflowers, their eyes pointing up to the sun.

The Eleventh

Colene Allen

She hated the smells and the noise most of all.

The smells were the worst. The crumbling basement of what used to be their comfortable and happy home had become a torture chamber. It was full of the nauseating odours of mould, the iron tang of blood, and the acidic sting of smoke and fuel. The smoke sometimes choked her and made her cough. One of the smells was very much like the smell from their fireplace, but much stronger. Her mouth tasted bitter, and sometimes she felt sick. She couldn't drink enough water to take away the taste. Mamma said they had to only drink a little water, not a big glass.

Every night, she had to do the same thing. As the sun sank on the horizon, her brother would pick up their blankets and her teddy bear, telling her that it was time to go sleep. He was lying, of course. She knew they wouldn't sleep. It was impossible to sleep through the noise of the explosions, both big and small. The sounds of those machines that flew over their home was both sudden and terrifying. Those flying machines suddenly appeared and disappeared as quickly as they came. The noises were loud and never stopped.

She laid out her blanket in the deepest corner of the basement, settled herself and her teddy bear down, and prayed that any moment now, all the noise and fear would stop. But, it never stopped. On and on the noise happened, night after night without end.

What scared her most was how their friends and neighbours were disappearing. She would see them during the day, during the brief times she was allowed to play in the yard. Then, she wouldn't see them again. Big people, little people. They all slowly disappeared, but she didn't know where they went. One day they were there, the next they were gone. Everyone else looked sad and angry after someone disappeared.

Many times, when she was playing in the yard, they would hear an explosion. Her brother would run to her, pick her up in his strong arms, and carry her into the basement. They would hide there until the explosions ended. Sometimes that would be soon, and sometimes it would take a long time. Sometimes, the explosions were really close and shook the walls of the basement. Those ones scared her the most.

It was hard to tell when the big explosions increased. The noise of the explosions blended together, making it impossible to tell if there were more of them than the night before. The explosions were endless. Every night with fierceness, and sometimes during the day. There were always more small explosions during the day, with most of the big ones at night.

This night started like all the rest of them had. When the sun sank below the horizon, the explosions started, and soon there were so many that it was impossible to tell when one ended and the next one began. The yelling and screaming she could hear outside had become normal too. All through the night it continued. She prayed for morning, when it would all stop. At least, it would stop for a little while.

But it didn't stop this time. The explosions continued well past when the sun rose. This time, she was sure the world was ending. Her world was ending. She wondered what would happen if she was in one of those explosions. Would her brother be with her? Her Mamma? What about Papa? She hadn't seen him in a long time. She wondered where he was and why Mamma always looked sad when someone said something about him.

Suddenly, the sounds changed. The explosions slowed. There were less of them. She could hear the echo of each explosion now, rolling like thunder over the forests until the sound faded away.

As the echo of the last explosion faded into silence, she looked up towards the small sliver of light above her in surprise and wonder. After a few moments of silence, she heard something she had not heard in a long time. She almost thought she was in a dream.

The birds began singing again.

After what felt like a long time, her brother took her hand and slowly guided her out of the deep crevices of the basement, towards the sunlight outside. In fear, she clutched her teddy bear close. The further she moved towards the sunlight, the more her eyes hurt from the bright light. She had to close her eyes and stop moving a few times before she was able to keep them open. Slowly, she crept out of the basement towards the front yard of what was left of their house.

When she slowly moved away from the ruins of their home, she looked up at the white clouds in the sky in wonder and amazement. The sunlight was so bright after the darkness of the basement that her eyes hurt for the first few moments. The birds were singing in chorus, a joyously happy song that she had not heard in so long that she had almost forgotten what a merry tune the birds could sing.

Looking around, she saw her mother running towards the house with open arms and smile as big as her teddy bear. She was scooped up into her mother's arms, teddy bear and all. Her mother held her tight and she felt safe and warm for the first time in so long.

On the eleventh hour of the eleventh day of the eleventh month The War ended.

The year was 2022.

The Day After Twilight

J.C. Fields

The man stood looking out a large picture window at the front of the old farmhouse. His gaze focused on dark clouds gathering on the north-western horizon as dawn turned to day on this late fall day. The owner of the farm, a woman in her mid-thirties, remained asleep on the sofa in front of the fireplace. A blaze still burned after being started by the man the previous night. Warmth from the flames kept the room comfortable compared to the howling wind and below freezing temperatures outside.

Before dawn, he built a fire in the kitchen's wood stove to get a pot of coffee going. From what he could tell, the old place appeared self-sufficient. A hand pump well in the kitchen, chopped wood on the screened-in porch at the back of the house, and a well-stocked root cellar provided the necessities. The cellar contained canned vegetables, fruits, and smoked cured meats. He knew someone was missing. Color pictures in the house displayed a large handsome man, his arm around the woman who slept on the sofa. Probably her husband.

Bad weather usually came from the northwest in this part of the Badlands. These clouds looked ominous. Dakota walked over to where the man stood and rubbed her muzzle against his pant leg. He reached down and scratched the German shepherd's head and said, "Storm's coming. I'd better stoke the fire or we'll all be cold."

As he finished re-stocking the wood next to the fireplace, he heard the woman stir. Lying next to the hearth, Dakota lifted her head and stared at the sofa's occupant.

The woman asked. "What time is it?"

The man shrugged, "Past eight, I reckon, not real sure. Storm's coming in. Clouds look like snow."

The woman looked toward the kitchen. "Do I smell coffee?"

"Yes, would you like some?"

She nodded and curled her legs under her and arranged the blanket to keep her warm.

After he returned and handed her the coffee, she looked up at him and smiled. She was a petite woman, with a natural beauty marred only by a deep tan and worry lines. This morning her long blonde hair was matted from her restless night on the couch, but her blue eyes still blazed with a determination and defiance. She said, "Thank you for helping me last night. Not sure what I would have done if you hadn't come along."

He shrugged and returned to stoking the fireplace.

She took a sip of the coffee. "This is good. Thanks. You never did tell me your name last night."

He stood and turned toward her. "No, I didn't. Jonathan McBride. Folks call me Mac."

"Mac," she said, "That fits you. My name is Amanda Grayson. But you already knew that, didn't you?"

He nodded and kept his gaze on the woman.

She watched the dog and smiled. "She's beautiful. What do you call her?"

"Dakota." He paused for a few moments. "Miss Grayson, what the hell are you doing by yourself way out here in the middle of nowhere?"

She sighed and stared into the fireplace. McBride noticed a tear slide down her cheek.

"I'm married. I wasn't alone until a few days ago. My husband and I bought this place before the financial crash. We've lived here ever since. He thought we could survive on our own until things got better. But they haven't, have they?"

"No." McBride shook his head. "Not yet."

She stood and wrapped the blanket around herself. After walking to the large picture window, she looked out and remained silent for a few moments. "Up until last summer, we had over twenty families living within a few miles of here. All of us thought we could start new lives, sort of a new hippie movement, reminiscent of the last century. You know, peace, love, self-reliance, and all that crap. We were all clueless about how difficult it would be to survive. Everyone wanted to basically hide out until the country's economy recovered. We all worked our small farms and learned to preserve fruits and vegetables. My husband raised cattle and chickens. The families even developed a small barter system. Josh and I traded eggs for fruit and vegetables. Life wasn't great, but we had it better than a lot of folks."

"Who's Josh?"

"My husband." She suppressed a sob. After taking a sip of coffee, she remained quiet for a few moments. Turning away from the window, her attention focused on McBride. "About a year ago, the raids started. First, it was a few cattle rustled from the Timpson's farm north of here. Then there was a home invasion. No one was hurt, but they took food and ammunition. We don't have a sheriff anymore. As you saw last night, the closest town is abandoned. My husband and a few others started patrolling the area on horseback. It actually worked for a while. Then one of the other husbands was ambushed one night, and..." After pausing for a few moments, she continued, "After the ambush, we all gathered for a meeting to decide our next steps. Five of the families decided to give up and head for Texas. We've never heard from them."

McBride nodded, "Not surprising. Texas closed its border. No Yankees allowed."

"That's what the rest of us told them, but they went anyway. For a while, we were left alone. Then about two months ago, the raids started again. My husband left with several other men two nights ago. He hasn't returned."

McBride tilted his head, "Who are they?"

She shook her head. "We don't know. They wear motorcycle helmets, leather jackets and red pants."

"Red pants," McBride raised his eyebrows. "Really?"

"Yes. Some have red leather chaps, but most wear red-leather pants."

McBride chuckled. "Red Legs. Jayhawkers. We're in what used to be known as Kansas."

"Yes, I know. Is that significant?"

He shrugged. "Don't know. I find it interesting they're dressing like a group that guarded this part of the country over two hundred years ago."

"What do you mean?"

"In 1862, during the Civil War, numerous bands of pro-Confederate guerrillas from Missouri made incursions into Kansas from time to time. They committed all kinds of atrocities. A group of Union supporters formed a band of men who wore red leggings and defended Kansas. They were known as Red Legs and sometimes Jayhawkers. The names stuck. These guys either know history or it's a coincidence. More than likely, they know history."

She stared at him. "Why are they preying on us?"

"You're squatters."

"We are not. We bought this land with cash. I don't understand."

"Not sure, then." McBride tilted his head. "It's just a guess. Maybe they're from around this part of the country. Did you say motorcycle helmets?"

She nodded. "They all ride motorcycles. No one can figure out where they get the gasoline."

McBride stared at her and grew quiet for a moment. Finally, he said, "I'm sure they have a source."

She studied him. "You drive an old Jeep, where do you get your gas?"

He shrugged. "Here and there."

She pressed her lips together and took a deep breath. "Are you one of them?"

He shook his head. "No. But I am from Missouri."

"Why did you help me last night?"

"Seemed like the right thing to do."

Dakota's head jerked up. She quickly got to her feet and moved swiftly to the front door. Her ears perked up, her tail horizontal and straight.

McBride said, "What is it, girl?"

The dog whined and barked twice. McBride turned to the woman, "Get in the basement. Now!"

He drew the Glock 22 he wore on his belt, checked to make sure a round was in the chamber and walked to the door. He touched his partner's head, "What's out there, girl?"

Dakota continued to whine and stood like a statue, not a muscle moved. She was concentrating on either a sound or a scent. McBride wasn't sure. He guessed a scent. The wind was blowing in from the northwest and the sky grew darker by the minute. Dust swirled and twisted around the front of the house. McBride strained to hear anything but wind.

Finally, he thought he heard revving motorcycle engines far off in the distance. He touched Dakota's head, scratched it gently, and said, "Sounds like we have company, girl. Let's greet them." Dakota looked up. McBride touched his nose and then a circling motion with his finger. He opened the door and Dakota sprang out and ran to the west of the house. He grabbed his coat from a hook next to the door. Before going out, he looked back into the room and saw Amanda standing in the living room holding a Remington pump-action shotgun.

He said, "Thought I asked you to move to the basement?"

"You did," she said. "I chose to get the shotgun."

McBride's mouth twitched. "Dakota's on scent and I'm going after her. Try not to shoot either of us when we get back." He opened the door and followed his partner out into the howling wind.

* * *

Amanda Grayson stepped to the front door. She watched as her rescuer from the night before followed his German shepherd out into the storm. He wasn't as tall as her husband. She guessed him to be a little over six foot tall.

Where her husband was built like a football player, this man appeared more like a runner. He wore his blond hair long, not quite on his shoulders. His six-or-seven-day old beard, blue jeans and flannel shirt gave him a rugged, handsome look. Not as handsome as her husband Josh, but still, she found him attractive. Josh was a big man. He also knew how to fight and survive. She couldn't believe—no, she wouldn't believe he might be gone forever.

Her thoughts turned to wondering what would have happened if the blond man had not appeared out of nowhere during her search for anyone who might know about Josh. She closed her eyes and shivered. The foul breath of the man who threatened her while the other two men held her would be hard to forget. But nothing happened. Pushing the image from her mind she said a quick prayer of thanks for McBride showing up when he did.

Snowflakes started blowing sideways as she stood at the door, shotgun ready if needed. She could distinctly hear motorcycles in the distance, despite the wind. She swallowed hard as her grip on the shotgun tightened.

* * *

McBride kept his eyes on Dakota twenty-five yards ahead. She continued to stop every few yards and test the air. He could tell she was following a scent, but the swirling wind made it difficult for her to determine the direction. He caught up and knelt next to the alert dog. Placing his right hand on her back, he felt every muscle in her toned body shiver as she tried to find the scent again. Finally, she relaxed, and he said, "Follow." She took off at a dead run. He watched as she headed north toward a road and disappeared into the wind-swept snow.

The motorcycles were closer now, their engines distinctly whining in the direction Dakota headed. Jogging toward the sound, McBride placed his right hand on the holstered Glock. He made a sharp one-note whistle as he ran. When he heard one bark in response, he knew he was directly behind Dakota.

The motorcycle engines went to idle, and the sudden silence gave him pause. He stopped and twisted his head in various directions trying to determine where they were. Muffled voices could be heard and then the engines revved several times. Suddenly the engines screamed as both vehicles accelerated away from McBride's location. As the sound of the bikes receded, McBride heard Dakota bark three times. He rushed toward the sound.

Within seconds, he could see the dog guarding a shape on the ground. As he drew nearer, the shape turned into a man. McBride said, "Back." Dakota turned her head toward him and immediately ran to his side. He slowed as he approached the prone figure, Glock drawn and pointed toward the ground, ready if needed.

The figure moved and moaned. It struggled to sit up. McBride saw the figure was a large man dressed in jeans and a dark-blue parka. He was bare-headed and when he turned in McBride's direction, he recognized him from a picture in the old farmhouse. It was Amanda's husband, Josh.

* * *

"They want us to leave. That's what they told me over and over. We have to leave. This was their land and we have no right to live here." Josh Grayson was sitting at the kitchen table drinking coffee and wolfing down eggs. Amanda stood off to the side having made the quick meal for her husband.

Her voice trembling, Amanda said, "How can they say that?"

McBride stood in the doorway of the kitchen, listening. Dakota was sitting quietly next to him. The man had been ambushed while on a patrol with two other neighbors. The gang had released Josh to convince the remaining farmers they had to leave, or the captured men would never be seen again. McBride said, "Where were you held?"

"The old county courthouse on Fifth and Merchant in Oswego. They're using the jail to hold everyone they have captured. Bob and Frank are still there."

"How many others?" McBride kept his gaze on the big man.

Josh drank more coffee. "At least seven. I didn't know them. They told me they lived west about fifteen miles. We're east." He looked at McBride. "What's going on here, Mac?"

"Not sure, maybe I should find out."

* * *

The snow squall blew past by noon. The landscape sparkled as sunshine reflected off three inches of fresh snow. McBride drove his well-maintained Jeep through the deserted streets of what was once the town of Oswego, in the forgotten state of Kansas. In his former life as a US marshal based in Missouri, he knew the town and the location of the courthouse, having picked up prisoners held by the sheriff's department numerous times. This knowledge also allowed him to know which streets to use to avoid being seen by anyone at the jail.

Even before the massive financial upheaval that ripped the country apart five years earlier, the town had been shrinking. Now it was completely abandoned. The shops and businesses were gone. In their place boarded-up buildings in disrepair stood everywhere. He passed the burned-out grocery store undoubtedly torched during the food riots which occurred shortly after the crash. The town had always depressed him. Now it only reminded him of how far this part of the country had declined.

The tracks his Jeep left in the newly fallen snow were evidence of his passing, but with the warm afternoon sun, they too would soon disappear. Dakota sat in the back of the Jeep, her head inches from McBride's right shoulder, her tongue hanging as she panted. An abandoned garage he knew about at Fourth and Merchant would give him a place to hide the Jeep. It had been vacant for as long as he had been traveling to Oswego. As he approached Merchant Street driving west on Fourth, he saw the building with the garage doors facing north. From this location, the county courthouse would be one block due south.

With the Jeep secured in the building and positioned for a quick exit, McBride noted the sun had finished melting the morning's snow. No Jeep tracks could be seen leading to the building. He and Dakota might be able to pull this off without being discovered.

As the two were exiting the building, McBride stopped. A motorcycle whined in the distance. Its direction masked as the sound bounced off walls of buildings in the area. He touched the top of Dakota's head and the dog looked up. With an open palm, he patted his right leg twice, the signal for Dakota to stay. After waiting for a few minutes, the sound of the motorcycle faded. When quiet returned, he signalled the dog to follow and they walked west on Fourth across Merchant to an alley just west of the old library.

Traveling down the alley, they passed the towns old water tower and made their way to Fifth directly across from the courthouse. Several motorcycles were parked around the front entrance, but the most prominent vehicle was a large tanker truck in the parking lot east of the courthouse. This would be the source of the group's gasoline. Feeling the need to view the scene closer, McBride returned to the back of the old fire station. He found an unlocked door and slipped inside. Standing still, he listened for the sounds of other occupants of the building. Hearing none, he knelt and took Dakota's head in both hands. He rubbed her neck and whispered, "Who's a good girl?" Dakota's tail wagged briskly, her tongue hung out as she panted and then licked his nose. He made a circling motion with his right index finger and Dakota headed off into the building to search for anything unusual or dangerous.

McBride made his way to the front of the station. The building had been picked clean by looters years ago. Thick dust lay everywhere and the one remaining fire truck was a skeleton of its former self. The only remnants being a metal body and flat, decomposing tires. Glass windows in the station's front doors gave him a perfect location to view the front of the courthouse. Dakota returned to his side. She whined and lay down next to him. The building was clear.

For over an hour, he watched in silence, seeing little activity. Occasionally, a man would exit the courthouse and walk to the corner of Fifth and Merchant. He would smoke a cigarette and look up and down the streets. McBride couldn't tell whether he was on guard duty or waiting for someone or something to arrive.

With sunset less than an hour away, he heard the rumble of a large vehicle approaching his location. His view to the west remained restricted by part of the firehouse, but he heard the familiar sound of air brakes as a tracker-trailer rig slowed to a stop on the street between his location and the courthouse. The truck bore no markings. The driver exited the cabin and waved to the man waiting at the corner. As they got closer to each other, they conversed in Spanish.

McBride had a rudimentary understanding of the language from his US marshal days. The conversation between the two men rapidly became disturbing the longer he listened. He patted his right leg once. Dakota stood and followed as he quickly left the old fire station.

* * *

By the time he returned to the Grayson's farm, the sun had dipped below the horizon and dusk faded. Amanda had a meal ready when he arrived, which he ate in silence. Both she and Josh waited patiently for him to reveal the details of his trip. His first words were to Josh. "How many families are still here?"

"Fifteen."

"How many are willing to defend their land?"

"All of us. Why?"

"We have to take the fight to the Red Legs."

* * *

The following night, Josh and two other men rode into Oswego in McBride's Jeep, with Dakota in her normal spot. They had a simple plan. McBride and Josh would work as a team, while Jason and Caleb had their own assignment. After McBride parked the Jeep in the same garage as the day before, they split up. Jason carried flares and Caleb held his deer rifle. They headed south toward the location of the parked fuel tanker. McBride, Dakota, and Josh returned to the alley and made their way to Fifth Street. When they arrived, McBride stood silently and listened. Off in the distance, the sound of a generator could be heard at the rear of the courthouse. He asked. "Did they have electricity when you were inside?"

Josh shook his head. "No. We only had candles at night."

McBride nodded. "The tractor-trailer rig brought more supplies to the group. They're establishing a base at the courthouse." He paused, his gaze sweeping the area. "They feel safe right now, I don't see any guards. Let's take advantage of this mistake."

They crossed Fifth Street and made their way to a row of motorcycles parked side by side. Josh removed a roll of cotton strips from his backpack. These were torn from old bedsheets donated by the families near Josh Grayson's farm.

He unrolled the cotton and handed one end to McBride. Josh then watched the ex-US marshal remove the caps from the fuel tanks of each motorcycle. At each bike, he placed a section of the cotton strip into the fuel tank.

At the last bike, McBride fashioned a much longer section of the roll and waited until Josh had moved behind the courthouse. He struck a match and lit the longer strip. Without hesitation, he hurried to Josh's location. The fire traveled up the length of cotton and disappeared into the tank. Almost instantaneously, the bike exploded in a ball of fire. Only seconds passed before the remaining bikes detonated into a catastrophic inferno. Satisfied with their work, they moved to find the generator and repeat the procedure.

The conflagration from the parked bikes became the signal for Jason and Caleb to complete their task. From their place of hiding, Jason ran and placed a lit flare under the tanker. He then made a mad dash back to where Caleb lay several hundred feet to the north. Just as Jason returned, they observed men hurrying out of the courthouse. As these individuals hustled to extinguish the fire around the bikes, Caleb fired his rifle at the tanker several times just above the burning flare.

The flare ignited the fuel from the now leaking tanker. When Caleb sent more bullets into the stainless-steel container, a massive explosion of burning gasoline erupted. Several of the men closest to the truck were engulfed as the fireball spread outward and upward. The tractor-trailer rig, now parked next to the tanker, was consumed in the fireball.

Pandemonium erupted as the survivors tried to determine what had happened. With Josh guarding the back door of the courthouse, McBride and Dakota entered through a rear entrance and headed straight for the jail. From previous visits, McBride knew its location. He used a small flashlight with a hand-cranked battery. It wasn't very bright, but it allowed him to navigate the dark halls of the building. With Dakota standing guard, McBride entered the jail area and found the remaining prisoners huddled around a table, light provided by candles, in the common area. They required very little persuasion to leave the building. McBride told them to follow

Dakota. He would remain behind for a few moments to make sure no one pursued them.

Just as he turned to leave, a bright flashlight was pointed at his face and a voice said, "Don't move."

His hand quickly moved toward his holstered Glock and the voice said, "I wouldn't." McBride brought his hand back in front of him and stood still. The flashlight grew closer and McBride raised his hand to shield his eyes. The voice said, "I take it you're the one responsible for the mess outside?"

McBride remained silent. The voice grew closer and said, "That wasn't very smart. You have no idea of who you're dealing with."

McBride smiled and said, "Oh, I know."

The man behind the flashlight raised his gun even with McBride's head. "Then you know what I gotta do."

Dakota leaped out of the darkness, her jaw clamping down on the man's gun arm. He screamed and dropped both the pistol and flashlight. While Dakota attacked the man, McBride grabbed the flashlight and un-holstered his gun. He pointed it at the man, who was now on the floor trying to defend himself against Dakota's attack. McBride said, "Back." Dakota immediately broke off and came to his right side.

McBride grabbed the man by the front of his shirt and yanked him to his feet. He placed the gun under his chin and said in a low growl, "I know why you're here. Tell your bosses, welcome to the Badlands." He lowered the gun and shot the man in the knee. He turned and followed Dakota out of the courthouse.

* * *

When McBride and Dakota emerged from the back of the building, they were greeted by Josh and one of the men just rescued, Frank Timpson. Josh grabbed McBride in a bear hug and Dakota let out a low growl. Josh backed off quickly and offered his hand, which McBride shook. Josh said, "We don't know how to thank you, Mac. Everyone is safe. Jason and Caleb have the survivors under guard at the fire station and we located our horses."

McBride nodded and smiled. "This isn't over, you know. There'll be others."

Frank frowned and said, "What do you mean?"

"I overheard a conversation yesterday. Someone wants the oil shale under your land."

"We'll be ready."

McBride smiled and said, "I hope so." He looked over where the tanker truck still blazed. "I have to go." He turned his attention back to Josh and said, "You folks take care."

Josh cocked his head to the side and said, "You never really told us why you are here."

"Heard a rumor someone I've been looking for was living on a farm in the area."

Frank said, "We know everyone around here. What's their name?"

"She's not here."

With those words, he shook both men's hands and patted his right leg once. Without looking back, he and Dakota jogged back to his Jeep.

Outside the Walls

A.L. Butcher & Diana. L. Wicker

Duchess Eleanor Reslin stood at the top of the city keep watching the amber rays of the newly risen sun over the crystal blue waters of the lake. The sight was breath-taking in its majesty, and she breathed in the cool, fresh air, thinking it was as glorious now as when she'd first set eyes on it. She'd missed it in the last few months.

Those who had once fled the discontent and unrest of the eastern lands called it the "Light of Hope" in the soft, lilting language of those who had first crossed the craggy rocks and deep snows to find this land. Now it was just the Golden Waters, probably more so for the gold brought into the city than the beauty of the sunrise. At this time of the morning, the sun was twinned in reflection, and Eleanor smiled to see its magnificence. There had not been much to smile about of late, but this sight filled her soul with joy. Whatever happened, whatever life brought the sun would rise and cast her light on the lake and bring this. She had to remember that.

The discontent in the lands beyond the valley from which the ancestors of these people had fled seemed to have followed them at long last. War had come, and with it, disease, poverty, fear and unease, and now they were banging at the gates.

The early morn had the chill of springtime and it whipped the woollen mantle about her shoulders. Cold air nipped her fingers, but this was the best vantage spot in the town, and so she stayed, rubbing her hands and wishing she had remembered to bring gloves. In the morning after her return, she had been so eager to look out on the city and the beautiful sunrise that it had slipped her mind.

As the shadows fell away beneath her, some of the areas seemed dingier than usual. There was a shadow over the docks, a sense of crowdedness she did not recall seeing before. Even the hovels seemed danker, more depressing, although at this distance it was not easy to tell. An unexpected movement caught her eye, and she turned towards the south, leaning over the battlements and squinting at what looked like coloured cloth flapping in the breeze. As the light continued to grow, her eyes narrowed and her jaw set. It was not just a cloth, but tents, lean-tos, wagons, and people huddled against the city wall. Perhaps more refugees from the war? There had been many of those of late, but Eleanor had not realised things were this bad. Perhaps the Council had not been as forthcoming as she thought.

The winter had been long and hard in the high valley, almost as if the mountains joined her in her mourning that no word had come from the battlefield before the snows set in. Winter was not a good time to be making war, but then again was there a good time for such endeavours? The Council had advised it would be over in a matter of months. It seemed they had been wrong.

Many of the citizens of Havenforth had perished and even within the palace, there had been losses from among the staff and the Duke's own regiment. Eleanor knew that had any word come, any at all, the Council would have found a way to get through to her. As no word had come, as soon as the road was even marginally passable from the Winter Palace to the pass, she had gathered those dearest to her and braved the remaining snow and ice to reach the hidden pass and follow its twisting turns to the city as spring began a tentative grasp on the lands. Eleanor had gone reluctantly to the Winter Palace, she had argued her place was among her people, but the Council had overruled her, and in His Grace's absence she had found herself with little choice. As she looked out over the city Eleanor decided it would not happen again. She was, in effect, Regent, but the Council consisted mainly of old men whose attitude was that a woman could not possibly rule. Eleanor was young but she was not a fool and her mother had ruled for a time in her own lands. There had been words between herself and the Council, but in the end, she had been persuaded to travel having been convinced her husband would soon return from his campaign.

Nodding to herself with an air of determination, she climbed down the iron stairs and wound her way to the chambers below, where the elderly chatelaine was busy coordinating the day with the staff. "Excuse me, Alys. What is wrong down in the working district, and why are there people outside of the walls? It is still so very cold out there."

"Hmm." Alys looked up from her books and waved the staff away. "Oh yes, I don't suppose you know of the decrees the Council has made since the snows blocked the pass, Duchess Eleanor. They've closed the city to more refugees. Overcrowding, they said. We can't feed all these new bodies, who contribute nothing to the city. There has never been this many asking for refuge, or so many beggars. It is not good for the city or the coffers, or so they said. Those who can help the farmers, herders, or fishermen are readily absorbed into those communities as the people follow the road from the pass. Those with specialized skills that can be used within the city are allowed in to work, but the rest..." She shook her head as she tisked. "I'm afraid they are locked out."

"Locked out? I don't think the gates have ever been locked in my husband's lifetime, or his father's, for that matter, or so he told me before he rode to battle. His Grace did leave orders to lock the gates if the battle came to our walls, but that was the last resort, to buy us time to get to the far valley or wait out a siege if that was the only option," Eleanor said, surprised. Something else the Council had neglected to mention on her recent return.

"In the early days everyone was allowed in and sent to the docks to find work: manual labour, cooking and...entertainment, things the unskilled do. There is always one ship or another looking to be unloaded, or manure to shovel. It doesn't take much to haul boxes or gut fish. Soon enough there were too many people and too little work and gates were shut on the district way-fares which the city guard patrol. There have been those who've tried to climb in, cut down from what I've heard, Your Grace. There is a curfew now; once the sun goes down, all good citizens must be behind closed doors or be on legitimate business. The keep dungeons are full of drunks, whores, and curfew breakers, the desperate and the hungry. Children too, so it seems. Crime is widespread. The desperate will steal if they are hungry enough. The hangman is the only one earning his keep these days."

The chatelaine shook her head at the situation. "Now even most of the traders stay within their ships and bring their own guards when they come to trade. If they come. I hear families from afar have stopped sending their sons to study, as well. Many domestics and skilled labourers were able to find rooms with their masters, which, I'm afraid, has only shifted the crowding into other districts, as now sometimes entire families huddle in one small room above a shop or below a kitchen somewhere. It's a shame, I've not known the like in all my years, but I am just a chatelaine, it is not my place to instruct the council," Alys concluded.

"What of those outside the walls?" Lady Eleanor asked, now angry and distressed at the situation.

"Oh, those by the caravan gate? Never you worry, the next trader to cross the waters will carry them on to warmer shores. They always do. Although..." A look of concentration crossed the chatelaine's face as her brows furrowed. "It seems to me that the traders have grown more infrequent of late. It could be they have been waiting quite a while."

"I see." Duchess Eleanor nodded grimly, not liking what she had been told. "I thank you for your candour, and for catching me up on the things I missed during the long winter, which the Council didn't feel fit to mention. I shall create a list of supplies to be prepared and then I shall require the great iron key set from the Duke's lockbox. I expect all to be ready after the household has broken their morning fast, and the steward to come to me when it is. This would not have occurred in the valley lands."

The chatelaine stood and bowed as the Duchess exited the chamber, wondering what was on her young mistress's mind. She had not known quite such a resourceful woman in the keep for some time. Not since the old Duchess had died and left the current duke's father bereft. Even Duchess Maria had not quite had the look Alys had seen on the young Duchess' face. Alys smiled – there would be trouble for the Council this day, she thought.

* * *

Eleanor carefully looked over the baskets and chests that had been lined up on the banquet table containing various herbs, tonics, medicinals, and easily carried foodstuffs from the kitchens – hams, bread, cheeses and even some apples. Old clothes, bandages, blankets and some tools had been found from among the keep supplies, basic supplies that could have been distributed before, but had not been. Eleanor herself had donated a couple of gowns, a wrap and a cloak or two and a long ream of linen she'd thought to use for something else. Now it seemed inconsequential. Nodding, she turned to the steward and held out her hand. "I thank you for your assistance. I cannot believe if His Grace were home that he would stand for such. It is hard to believe, in a city of scholars and artisans, that none are familiar with the construction of a simple home, let alone a basic hovel. The winter has been harsh, even within the walls. I only hope we are not greeted by cairns along the walls or the Council will not wish to hear the words I will have for them."

Taking the ring of large, iron keys, she strung it through her leather belt. "Have a servant and that errand boy— Thomas, isn't it—waiting with the pony and wagon at the head of the high street. We shall join him shortly."

Eleanor paused at a looking glass as she strode down the central hallway. The face in the mirror looked tired and worn, for the journey had been long and unpleasant and what she had found on her return was not good news. Her complexion was pale, and dark circles hung under her eyes. She was thin and the anxiety clouded her face. Yet her shapely jaw was set determinedly and her eyes held steel.

She had looked forward to a hot bath and long sleep, but such luxuries could wait. Her work was far from over.

She pulled a woollen hat of forest green over hair of dark plum and found a scarf of black silk, a gift from the Duke. As she wound it about her neck, her fingers brushed the silver amulet nestled in the hollow of her throat. For a brief moment after speaking with the chatelaine, she had considered opening the large trunk in her chamber and shaking out the ceremonial robes of state, which she had been given for official visits within the city, but then she had thought better of it. Such garments were not suited to the job at hand, so she had simply donned clean travel clothes of sturdy, warm wool and joined her companions at the morning meal.

Her cousin and confidante Lynette, and Gavin, the young captain of her personal guard, were sitting close together. One playing his lute softly, for he was a musician as well as their protector, and one listening in rapt attention, as Eleanor stopped by the parlour, having sent for her favoured companions.

Seeing Duchess Eleanor in the doorway, Lynette patted Gavin's arm as she stood. "Cousin, we've been waiting for you. Something is afoot?"

Lynette was petite, like Eleanor, but darker of colouring, her brown hair with mahogany highlights perpetually worn in a long braid, and her skin olive. She had given up her life in their distant town when His Grace had taken Eleanor to wife. They were as close as sisters, and Lynette was no mere companion. While she possessed no magic of her own, as Eleanor did, Lynette's skill with obtaining rare ingredients from both flora and fauna made her poultices and potions the envy of even the most skilled apothecaries in the city.

Gavin carefully set aside his lute, trading it for a sword which he belted over his colours, the black and gold of the House of Reslin. Rarely did he don his official surcoat which marked him for what he was, but he did not like the changes he had heard about in town as he chatted with the household staff. It paid to be prepared. He was known well enough among those of rank in most circles to not need to advertise, so the crest upon the scabbard and the black and red woven sash over his leather armour was usually enough to alert others that he was a member of the Duke's household and a Summoner-Blade. Gavin thought such behaviours within the city would never have been tolerated by the Council if his Grace had been here. The war had lasted longer than anyone had anticipated. Gavin had wished to attend his liege, yet followed his duty when commanded to protect the Duchess. There were others of his order with the Duke, Gavin hoped it was enough. Of course, Lynette was here, an added bonus, and from the accounts he had managed to get the war had taken its toll. Perhaps they would both have fallen if they had travelled with the army. Gavin was not sure he could survive life without her.

"Gavin," Eleanor sighed. "I thought I said I wanted to travel unnoticed today. How are we supposed to do that if you're flashing the castle's colours about the town?"

"Ah, ye of little faith, my dear lady." He smiled and winked as he slung a grey cloak about his shoulders and donned a wide-brimmed hat with a large plume on one side. "Now, I am merely a handsome young buck escorting two lovely ladies on a stroll, who just happen to be followed by a wagon of goods. Set that cloth of yours on top and we will look like we've been shopping and decided to wander about with our purchases in tow."

"Hmm," murmured Lynette as she held a black cloak lined with ermine out for Eleanor. "I'm not sure I see you as a young buck, more a roguish rake likely trying to gain our favour. Or the hired sword of our master protecting two ladies and his goods. That is hardly inconspicuous."

"Are you certain this is a good idea, Eleanor?" Lynette asked.

"I'm banking on the fact that the guard would not expect me to be walking through the poorer parts of town. After all most of them have never seen me close up." Eleanor hoped her plan would work, however should it not Gavin was well able to defend her.

"Truth be told, I'm more interested to see if anyone says anything when I open that gate," Eleanor replied as she fastened her cloak, smiling grimly at her two companions as Gavin held Lynette's cloak and kissed her lightly on the cheek.

* * *

They travelled as far as the city's heart, the great central gardens already bursting forth with colour from the many exotic plants gifted from the faraway lands whose traders visited this city of artistic and scholarly endeavours. As they passed through the gardens, pleasantries were exchanged but a few people gave curious glances at the wagon and its goods. As Eleanor had hoped no one expected the lady of the land to be wandering the streets and thus no one seemed to realize who greeted them that morning.

"Someone's been to market early today, I see," one passer-by remarked to another. "You'd think they'd at least send the lad and the wares on to his master instead of flaunting them about, with all these cutpurses."

"If I were the lad, I'd be certain not to arrive home without my mistress. All the better to have her loveliness distract from the stamped notes that are sure to arrive later to claim a fair share of coins from her husband," the other snickered as Lynette paused, pushing her hood back just enough to smile coyly at the gentlemen.

A cough behind her ear and a hand on her elbow drew Lynette's attention away from the gossips. "Now there, none of your tricks, minx," Gavin said a little louder than necessary. "Right in front of the lad, you would look to pick someone up? And with your mistress at hand...One cannot get demure help these days," He tsk-tsked loudly at her, masking his smirk as the elder gentlemen hurried away.

Lynette jabbed him hard in the midriff. "You are in so much trouble when we get back..." she hissed.

"Must you two carry on so?" Eleanor questioned as she rolled her eyes at them. "I thought we were trying not to draw attention."

"Just shooing the gawkers away before they started wondering which husband had been fleeced of his coin at the market this fine morning." He smiled as he winked at her, flaunting his privilege of rank and friendship. "It's all part of the disguise."

Eleanor rolled her eyes again. "I do not know why I brought you along. Move on, will you."

Gavin bowed, noting the slight smile which crept upwards at the edges of her lips. "As you wish, m'lady."

They passed without further incident to the wide, main street that bisected the city. At one end the southern gate opened to the Golden Way, the great caravan highway paved in the worthless stones from the mountains that glimmered like gold and fooled the untrained. The Way snaked across the high ground of the plain to the only large mountain pass known to those from the lands beyond. This would be the way the refugees from the great war had travelled, seeking sanctuary.

Reaching the spiked iron gate, they saw a chain the width of a woman's wrist binding the bars. The lock was the size of a dinner plate; hefty, old and stiff. It would not be picked easily even if one did manage to creep past the guards. Eleanor was relieved they had not brought down the thick inner portcullis but said nothing. She strode over, as though she owned the town, which technically she did, and struggled with the large key until through force of will the lock clicked open. Gavin pushed the gate, hearing the rattle and creak of old, badly maintained ironwork.

Two beefy men ambled over from the guardhouse beside the gate. Their accent belied the fact that they were mercenaries from the lands across the sea and not the usual city guard. "Here now, what do you think you're doing? How'd you get that lock opened? Nobody exceptin' the captain is supposed to have a key to that!"

"Your livery is soiled," Duchess Eleanor replied as she looked the men over slowly. "You do your master no credit when you represent him dressed such. How far the city guard has fallen while their master has been away. You disgrace this town and yourselves. Where are the usual guards?

The elder guard shrugged. "What business is it of yours, woman? Gone to war, gone to the tavern, gone to the whorehouse. Who knows, it's just us today.

The younger of the men let his eyes roam over her, "O' course, miss, we could make ... enquiries if it were worth it. Depends what's on offer."

Eleanor looked the man down, "I doubt you have much to please a woman if your manhood is as feeble as your wit."

Pushing the gate wide, Eleanor turned to Gavin and handed him the iron ring of keys. "Stay here and ensure the gate remains open, no matter what it takes. Ensure this ... man, is relieved of his duty. I am sure the Regent would agree."

Looking through she continued grimly "We may not be alone when we return. I will send word if you are needed."

The guards started to move forward, as though thinking to intervene and prevent this interfering woman from her business, one hand on their swords. Gavin just shook his head, the index finger of the hand holding the keys wagging at them as he tossed the hat aside. The shadow beneath his feet began to spread, slowly rising as a purplish-black cloud about his legs. He let the cloak casually fall, revealing his colours. "I believe the Regent of Havenforth would prefer that you go clean yourselves up, but if your captain would like to speak with me, he's welcome to wander down to the gate. Of course, if you wish to challenge the Regent's personal guard and her tour of the town..."

The two men began to back away slowly, one shaking his head vigorously as the shadow reached out and grabbed his arm. "Before you go, perhaps you'd care to tell me what may have become of the old guards?"

* * *

Thomas and the servant led the wagon through the gate in the wake of the two determined women. To their left, a veritable shanty town existed in the shadow of the wall to the water's edge. Shelters built of discarded refuse housed an untold number of refugees, banished and forgotten by a city of plenty. Thin goats bleated, moving among the carts and tents, foraging for food. Udders barely providing enough to feed the few kids among them. Small wild-eyed fowl pecked at unseen scraps, competing with pigeons and rats, all of whom could be on the menu for those hungry enough. Feral dogs watched like wolves until scared away, lurking beneath the ramshackle dwellings, awaiting their chance to grab something.

Hearing the rumble of the wagon, a few elders exited the nearest hovel and approached. "You are not of the lost and useless." The first elder smiled as she bowed to them. Her hair was grey, and the stick upon which she leaned was nought but an old tree branch picked up along the way. About her shoulders was a moth-eaten blanket worn as a shawl, and Lynette was shocked to see her feet were bare and bandaged.

"And you do not look to be the sort that would be considered of no use to those within the walls," said a second old man. His garb was rough, patched in more than a few places, but Eleanor could see it once had been fine. He held himself erect, even in such a dire place. A man of means, fallen as many others had to the spectre of war. These folks were too old for arms, too old for labouring and of no 'use' to the city, mere bellies to feed, that much was plain.

Eleanor nodded to the elders and gestured to the wagon. "Elders, we come to offer what comfort and aid we can this day. Foodstuff, blankets and herbs, minor potions and salves. It is not much but perhaps it will help to ease your burden. We have some knowledge of herb lore, perhaps you have sick to attend?"

She looked around the myriad of faces, some dark and swarthy like the eastern men, others fair-haired and appearing more like the local folk. How far had the tide of war flowed and how many had it taken?

"How come such a variety of souls come here?" Eleanor asked, seeing a mix of faces and wondering how they all came to such a state as this.

Another elder shook her head. "We hail from many places, and all have travelled far to escape the hardship and famine left in the wake of the flowing tides of war. Those who gather here simply search for a place to call home and food to fill their bellies. Many of us have lost everything to the pillaging forces and the dark magic they bring. Those guards atop the walls bid us wait for the coming ships to take us to the warmer lands, or away from here, but no ships have come these past two full moons. More refugees come every day and the situation worsens."

"Come." One elder smiled, holding out her hand. "Share our meagre hospitality. It is the least we may offer for your generosity. Then you will see."

A dirt floor and ratty boards covered with old, threadbare rugs and rotting reeds greeted them as they entered. This hovel was barely large enough to contain them all. They took seats on the floor around a small circular table, which was little more than an old barrel. A young girl, clothed in ragged breeches and a well-patched shirt brought in a small wooden bowl of frothy goat's milk while a lad carried a wooden tray of slender golden oat-cakes. A thin wedge of yellow cheese and a tiny pat of butter followed, supplies hoarded, perhaps the last, but offered to guests in friendship. These people had lost much but still they gave what they had.

"Please partake. We do not have much, but what we have we share in good hospitality. We look out for each other here, for it takes the diligence of all to ensure survival outside the walls," One elder said, motioning to the food.

The oat-cakes were surprisingly good, perhaps sweetened with honey, and the milk was rich. Both women were touched by the generosity of these folks who had so little. "These are lovely," Lynette told them politely. "They remind me of a treat Mother used to make when I was small, but what of the children?"

Before she could hear the answer a haggard-looking, middle-aged woman burst into the hovel, dropping to her knees beside the elders. "Help us! Oh, please, you must help! It is my daughter. The baby is coming, but it is too soon! Our wise woman had given her herbs before to try and delay things, on the road when we were travelling, but she did not make it this far with us. The guards would not send for anyone last I asked. We've no coin for bribes nor aid. They were...unkind and uncaring. Perhaps they will listen to you, or you may send for help?"

Eleanor looked to Lynette, who gave a short nod. "My cousin is trained in herbs and potions. While we are not midwives, our boy can fetch one and send for the town apothecary. He will have the same sort of herbs as your wise woman and if he cannot delay, then our midwife here is skilled, she has saved many a child others could not. And should it be needed, I can ask for the aid of the Mother

Goddess herself. She has been known to heed my call from time to time."

Lynette stepped from the hovel and motioned to the servants. "Run and tell Summoner-Blade Captain Gavin that we need a midwife to tend to an early birth and have the master apothecary send a fast runner and a couple of apprentices with the proper supplies. He will know whom to call upon. Go quickly now, Thomas," she told the lad, who scurried off on his errand.

Eleanor followed the distraught mother from the hovel and paused before the servant at the wagon. "Distribute the food and blankets. Perhaps one of the elders can advise who among these people is most in need. Make sure the children receive something. There is a pouch of coins; there should be enough to buy more bread and supplies if needed. Follow their lead in our absence. We will send for you if you are needed." The servant gawped as Eleanor held out her silken purse containing what to her was small change but to those with nothing was a fortune indeed.

Grabbing a satchel of basic medical supplies and the warmest blanket, the ladies followed the anxious woman through the refugee encampment, past a gathering of battered, dilapidated wagons to the clusters of rag-tag tents crafted from scraps and cast-offs that barely fended away the damp chill blowing in off the lake. The pregnant lass was pale, shivering, and obviously frightened. Dropping her bag on the floor, Eleanor knelt beside the girl and took her hand. "We have sent for the midwife, she will be here soon. Try not to be too afraid, she is the best in the land. If you can manage some food that will bolster your strength. You'll not be alone."

Lynette gently touched the mother's arm. "What is your name, mistress? How many moons have passed?"

"Etelka," her mother whispered. "I am Etelka; she is Marla. Moons? More than six, perhaps seven..." She rubbed her face with her hands as she tried to think. "I can't remember, but I know we're not near to the eighth full moon yet. Everything has been so difficult, always on the move, never enough to eat. Our men died trying to protect the stores. The village had buried the winter stores in the forest, but the invaders came and..."

"I know, good mistress, I know," Lynette soothed. "Your daughter needed help, and you have found it. Now we need to think of the little one that may yet carry a lost name forward. I see you have no fire here. Where do you cook? Is there anywhere to find hot water or broth? I can make a tea that will help her relax. It may not be labour." Lynnette held out a small, cast-iron kettle in which she had already placed a few herbs, but more advanced potions would require the supplies from the apothecary. She hoped the shop-keep would not be stingy when he sent his youth with supplies.

"Yes, there is always a brazier among the wagons. We take turns filling the pots by the lake, and the men keep a safe fire, so it does not spread among the fabrics and dry wood. I have seen the black marks on the walls where a fire spread once before. Sometimes there is a communal cauldron, if there is any food to be had. Though the broth is meagre and the bread is stale and mouldy," the soon-to-be grandmother told her.

"I have not the herbs with me to attend to this need. It was not something we planned. I can, perhaps, ease the fever and calm her fear. I can see what the apothecary sends when the apprentices arrive with supplies. Hopefully, they arrive quickly or we will be passed the point of a potion's aid. If only we'd known..." Lynette said to Eleanor quietly.

With a glance at the tent, Lynette shook her head. This was no place to bring a new life into the world. It would likely be the end for mother and babe in conditions such as this.

Lynette grabbed the first woman she found close by as she made her way, swiftly towards the fire and thrust a couple of coins into her hand. "Fetch soup, broth, anything nourishing and take it to the faded green tent. There'll be another coin for your trouble when you return."

Bustling off before the surprised woman had a chance to respond, Lynette returned to their supply wagon only briefly, giving orders to the servant to fetch a goodly swath of the clean linen to his mistress in the far tent, and to pay those folk kind enough to bring food to the tired, pregnant lass. Anyone who donated clothes and blankets would be recompensed.

Word had spread about the donated food and so she had to weave her way through the poor and hungry. Hands thrust out, desperate, and hungry mouths pleaded. Lynette knew they had not brought enough, they simply hadn't known. Want was everywhere among these lost and destitute folk. For a while, she grasped the dagger at her belt while she walked, worried someone would accost her hoping for coin or other handouts, but most simply stared at the small figure with her good, warm cloak and her sturdy boots, or nodded in vague acknowledgement. Although these people were in such need there was not the stampede she'd feared. Thieves were rare – there was nothing to steal.

The caravans and wagons clustered against the wall were old and battered, and a few looked as though they had once been properly enclosed, but the walls appeared to have been chopped away. Others bore the rusted metal arches of canvas supports, no doubt the same ragged canvases that were strung above them from the wall itself, providing a canopy for those who huddled close to the fire pit. Nearby, the remnants of upturned wagons formed makeshift shelters for bodies bundled under old furs and dingy cloth. Lynette hoped none here carried any ailment that was sure to spread quickly through such a gathering of people. The plague was a real risk, but these poor folks had little choice. Any plague might even spread to the city within. It had been known before.

An old man, bent and broken with a cloth wound over one eye and a wooden peg strapped where his right leg had once been, sat on an upended log beside a large cast-iron cauldron. He touched his fingers to his temple as she approached, much like a soldier's salute.

"Pleased I'd be if you'd forgive me my manners, miss, but as you can see, I'm not much for standin' these days. If we were t'other side o' the pass, I'd say you were from the Ladies' Aid, but this city hasn't shown no mind for such acquaintance. 'Tis a shame really, for sure and it looks to me like they could certainly afford such."

Shaking his head, he ruffled the scraggle of grey hair sticking up above his bandage. "But I go a ramblin' on, when you've come here with a pot in hand. No doubt you'll be a bit o' the hot water then? We just ask for a trade, a bit o' this 'n for a bit o' that. If 'n you've got anythin' that may be useful to the world-weary, we'd be most obliged if you'd share it."

Lynette heard mumbling from the large figure lying in the shadow of one of the wagons, and she started to step closer, trying to make out his words, distracted by what might once have been a pattern on the dingy cloth, a hint of red and black among the grime and dried blood. She saw the edge of a cloak, now little more than ragged shreds, and it looked strangely familiar; a hint of gold trim, and the barest flash of silver from something at his throat. The kind old man took the pot from her hands and filled it as she stared past him. He inhaled deeply the fragrance of the herbs as the hot water rehydrated them.

"An apothecary, is it? Well, now... When you've finished tendin' what you're doin', perhaps you'll come back by then, eh? I'm certain sure Himself over beneath the wagons and his friend might benefit from a touch o' something. One's a cripple, like I, and the other calls for someone in his fever. Old soldiers what fled the war and has yet to find a welcome," the old man said as he passed her filled pot back to her.

"Leena," a hoarse voice rasped from the shadows. Someone crawled from beneath the pile of skins beside another wagon and pulled themselves along the ground to his side. The lad's legs were useless and sheer determination and love of his friend pulled him along to tend his companion, who moaned softly in the delirium of his fever. The young man, barely out of his youth with haunted eyes and a haggard expression, gently stroked the prone figure's hair. They had obviously endured much together. Beneath the filth on the crippled man's garment, Lynette was certain she recognized the colours, and she swallowed the stirring she felt would choke her as she nodded to the kindly old man.

Lynette caught the boy, Thomas, returning from his errand and said, "Run and fetch Gavin and a good sturdy wagon or cart. One fit to carry a man. Send him to Her Grace, as fast as you can."

* * *

The midwife was a large, no-nonsense figure in swirling skirts and sturdy boots. Those eyes had seen more than most, both of life and death and life again, and those hands had brought into the world more souls than she cared to admit. Arriving at the Caravan gate, she paused to take in the scene before her. A group of burly men huddled in the dust of the great roadway as misty figures swirled about them. The cries of the men mingled with the wails of those who tormented them, and the midwife rolled her eyes and shook her head. "I thought all the sorcerers had departed with the Duke, to go to war," the midwife muttered, eyeing the cloaked figure who summoned the shadows.

Before the gate, Gavin stood nose to nose with the new captain of the city watch, a man who had barely made lieutenant when Gavin had seen him last, although his arrogance was much the same. The guard tapped the circlet of silver he wore on his brow. A large oval of yellow agate was set upon a sliver of black obsidian and rested upon the centre of his forehead, a ward against restless spirits and dark thoughts. "Your summoning won't work against me. The scholars know your business as well as you do, necromancer. I was the only man among the city guard that knew the Council to be right. There will be none of your old mates coming to assist you this day, most are worm food and just as well. Dabbling with the dead and spirits from the nether realms, it ain't right," snapped the captain, tired of this charade.

"It looks to me that none of your sell-swords will be aiding you either," Gavin sneered. He could just as well run this man through for his insolence but the city was in enough turmoil as it was. He could wait.

Carol, the midwife, looked the guard captain up and down and snorted at the posturing men. She had little time for such masculine displays, such foolishness had started this war now banging on the city gates. "Frederick Hilary Ormson! You always were one to be awkward, even as a boy. I see nothing has changed 'cepting now your sword is real. I brought you into this world, boy, and I smacked your arse when you gave your poor mother trouble. I'll do it again, don't you doubt it! Did you not think to fetch me to assist a woman in her need? They pays what they can afford, or they pays in kind. That is the way it is, and always has been. If some fool had thought with his purse and not his heart, you'd not be here now, nor that babe of yours neither. Now get you out the way, silly boy!" With that she swept past, as the embarrassed captain stood aside, humbled by the tirade and far more afraid of this woman than the Summoner-Blade. He mumbled something to be rebuked sharply with, "And I ain't deaf, neither."

In short order, Carol arrived at the appropriate tent, residents of the camp helpfully pointing her along the way as word of her upbraiding of the most feared of the city guards preceded her. Handing the steeping herbs to the midwife, Lynette asked if Eleanor would be needed further, and received an abrupt, but not unkind dismissal. "There are plenty here to tend if you've the skill, from what I've seen. I will call if I need another pair of hands. You have done what you can for her."

Lynette nodded, grateful and relieved. She pulled Eleanor away. "Let the midwife do her duty. There are others for you to see, and an apothecary's apprentice for me to find."

Outside, Eleanor said with a soft voice filled with anger, "They've been on the move for so long with so little. I fear we've come too late. There is so much that should have been done, could have been done..."

"And it will be done now, under your watchful eye, my lady. Where the fire is, where I got the hot water, there's a man suffering from a fevered dream. I really think you should go to him."

Eleanor shook her head. "What about those here? There are plenty who need us."

Lynette grabbed her arm, suddenly very serious. "Please, I really think you should tend to him. He's...a man from our army, one of our own. Your touch is much more tender than mine, and he may not have the time to wait. He needs the blessed touch of our Lady Mother."

Eleanor looked at the hand on her arm and the strange intensity in her cousin's face. "What about the others?"

Two wiry lads with small wooden cases slung across their chests arrived, looking somewhat confused. "The master says we are to give Her Grace whatever is required?"

Almost shoving her towards the wagons, Lynette said, "I really need you to listen to me. Go and tend that fever. Now I'm able to aid this lass properly. Boy, bring that box over here and let us see if we can convince the wee babe to wait another two moons to arrive."

* * *

Eleanor stopped just outside of the cluster of wagons and shifted the satchel slung over her shoulder, containing linen for bandages, a few poultices and salves, honey and herbs for infection and even poppy juice to dull the pain, or if needed end it. The second apprentice hung back and just stared at the sick and injured clustered under the wagons. He had never seen such wounds or misery.

'So much need,' she thought. Where did she even start? She wondered at Lynette's strange behaviour. Why was this man so special? She'd seen a few old soldiers already, mostly tending infections, the usual battle sickness, and once a younger man with his arm cleaved at the elbow.

The one-legged old man looked up from the fire and started, as though perhaps he had been nodding in sleep and failed to notice Eleanor's arrival. "Are you the apothecary? I thought the other lass might be returning after a while," he asked, eyeing her satchel. "You brought food for us? Give some to the cripple yonder and his mate, they needs it more 'n I."

"I?" Eleanor paused. "Lynette said there was someone with fever that needed tending. I've come to offer assistance until more healers from the town arrive. I have some healing magic of my own, plus bandages and some poultices."

"Ah, well and truly, you both must be the Ladies Aid, or the Blessed Mother's girl, but you'll be finding no healers to be a coming. We've called for 'em before. Can't pay, see?"

Eleanor watched as he scooped water into a battered tin cup and held it out for her to take before pointing to the mound of ragged cloth bundled in the shadow of the far, upturned wagon, knowing she would need it to clean wounds and mix herbs.

"They will come now or feel my wrath," she murmured, the anger bubbling within.

Feeling in the lining of her cloak, she pulled out a handful of coins, not a fortune but more than this fellow had seen in many a moon. Fetching a loaf of bread from her satchel, she broke it into pieces and handed both the coins and bread over. "For your kindness, Grandfather. There is food on yonder wagon, when I am done I'll send the lad to bring you something."

She stepped over to the forms huddled in the shade beneath the upturned cart. It was cold out of the sun and she supposed most of the passers-by had ignored these stricken forms, even if they had the means to help them. Often minds refused to behold what the eyes saw. Ignore a problem long enough and hopefully, it would depart, wasn't that said? The crippled youth looked into the face of the woman who crouched close to his friend. She had a radiance about her, and a kindness which had been rare these last few months. Something about her was familiar, but he could quite not place what. Perhaps she just reminded him of better times, of the girls at home and the times before the war. Her hands found the pitiful pile of blankets and gently unwrapped them.

"Can he drink? This will ease his fever. There is much infection here. Did the battle medics not think to tend him?"

"Oh, aye, m'lady, but I'll warn you; he's a sight to see. The war was cruel, what it took from us, from him. So much lost to us, even most of the battle medics and the mages. They lost plenty too, but we were, are outnumbered. Their magic from the depths of the seven hells, slew rank on rank of men. He fought with honour, though, and he did not desert his men. Even at the end, even when he fell, my lord kept on fighting until the magic and the wounds overtook him. I've never seen one take so much and still be breathing, slight though it is."

With slow and gentle practice, the young man lifted the bandaged head and brushed aside the matted hair and scraggly remnants of beard that erupted from the knobby scars across his face. A ravaged countenance marred with drying blood, infection and misshapen by magic. Once he had been handsome, now he was little more than a dying ruin of a man. His arm was bandaged, twisted and his frame thin and gaunt.

In the dark shadows of the wagon, it was hard to make out more than a shape, but she saw Lynette had been correct. This man was a soldier, there was a broken sword at his side and he had, once, perhaps had the build of a warrior. They both had been in the war, for the other wore a ragged medal, which despite their need he had not the heart to sell. The dying man stank of blood, infection and worse. Someone had tended him, bound the worst of his wounds but still, he was a shell of the warrior he once had been. Inwardly Eleanor wept for this man, his friend, for them all.

This was hardly the ideal place for healing, but then she thought grimly, it seldom was. Those who needed such magical healing tended to be in dire straits so she must make the best of it. The man was soaked in sweat, muttering and moaning. She took his hand and trying not to cry at this wreck of a man, she brushed her skin on his. "Mother-Goddess Saule, give me the strength and blessing to heal this man. Take his pain, take his wounds."

Gently she pulled open his ragged, blood-splattered cloak and saw the glint of silver Lynette had seen. About his throat was an amulet, silver twisted in an eternal knot, and in the centre was a dark and rare stone she knew so well. This was her gift to him, one summer day before he went to war. Then she saw the colours he wore, as her cousin had done beneath the filth. This was not just a man of her army, it was *her* man of the army.

"Mother, save him! Take my life if a life you want but spare him!" She could barely see through her tears and touched the pendant at her neck, also silver, a match to his. Soft white light weaved from her fingers, and she felt his pain, the terrible drain of magic spent and body broken. Washing his wounds and binding him in a magical web, which grew steadily brighter, stronger, she felt it tug at her, felt her strength ebbing, and the web of her gifts softly circled them both. Magic could heal and it could save, but such gifts were not assured. It might be too late, the wounds and magic loss too great. Even a battle sorcerer is mortal, and what price had he paid on that field of war against his enemies? How much of him was given? He would need time, hope, and care. Far more than he had received beyond these walls.

Exhausted she carefully pressed the cup to his lips as the youth held his head, saying softly, "Please drink this, my love. It will ease your pain. Give you some strength. Slow sips. It's poppy juice and honey, with herbs, rosemary, yarrow and peppermint."

"Leena?" His voice trembled. Those hazel eyes she knew so well flickered open, suddenly intense despite being fever-bright. A pale and scarred hand gripped hers with surprising strength. If she needed any more confirmation, she saw the thin band of gold he wore, etched with her name in the language of the old tongue.

Her fingers stroked the scars crossing his face. He was still handsome to his wife. She was not repelled as some would be, had been. With tenderness, she wiped his brow, and whispered in his ear, "My husband, my duke, how come you to this?"

Anger filled her, anger that any man in such a state, let alone the lord of the land, could be left this way, left to die, left in pain simply because he was outside the gates. What of the crippled soldier? This young man who'd tended his lord with such devotion. How many more? Her other hand found that of the young man and she held him too, this loyal soldier who had stayed with his liege, despite it all and despite his crippling wounds.

Hearing the tell-tale rumbles of several carts nearing, and the excited chatter of the refugees as the carts passed, Eleanor called out loudly, "Gavin! Gavin, is that you? Do you have the healers? Gavin, you must see this!"

Heavy footfalls told her it had been Gavin passing, and soon he was kneeling beside her. "M'lady? This is not a pregnant lass..."

Eleanor held up the charm for Gavin to see. "No, it is the Duke, my husband, left outside his own city gates. Left like refuse. Help him into the wagon, with the old man and the crippled boy too, who has been so kind. Take them to the keep. Then find others for any who cannot walk. If the merchants will not give their wagons or horses freely then commission them to the service of Duke Zander and Duchess Eleanor, tell them they will be recompensed, if that is all they care for. Fetch any with herb lore or a hint of healing and those who do not have it can provide food and blankets. I want the gates lashed open until every soul is inside. This is my edict as regent. If the Council refuses, then they shall be disbanded, and I shall choose my own. How many more have been lost because they could not pay or were inconvenient? We will no longer turn away those in need. If needs be, we will house them in the courtyard or the gardens, or even the keep itself until they are fit to work or fit to leave."

Gavin opened his mouth to protest, then, seeing the look of determination on her face, decided against it. Such fire had he seldom seen. Instead, he laid his cloak upon the cart and gently settled his lord on it. Zander groaned, muttering the name he knew, his hand clasping her soft one. "I am here, you're home," she whispered.

Walking close beside the wagon, head held high and one hand in his, she let them see him and the strength they shared. Gavin was shocked. His lord had been a big man, yet now he weighed barely more than Eleanor or Lynette. Yet he saw the look of love in her eyes, the steely will which would not yield. She would nurse him with her own hand, and she would save him or die trying.

* * *

The autumn sun was crimson as it rose over the Golden Waters, staining them blood red. It was a fitting dawn for the memorial in the central gardens of the city. Eleanor leaned out over the battlements as she had a few months past and breathed in the cool air. Fluttering fabric caught her eye, and the bustle of bodies in the city even at this early hour reminded her of that day. Yet *this* day was very different. Tents, canopies and pennants lined the streets, wagons and caravans formed a circle, and a wooden stage was peopled with troubadours and acrobats. Today was a festival day.

Eleanor turned back and clambered down the iron staircase, which someone had decorated with ribbon. Standing before the mirror, she was pleased to see her complexion returned to its soft, delicate form as she slowly combed her plum-dark hair, now with a hint of grey. The last few months had been taxing; there had been many heated discussions with the Council, a treasury already strained by war further strained by an uneasy and expensive peace and the recovery of many broken souls. But what were a few grey hairs for the price of peace and the safety of a town?

As she wriggled into the crimson robes of state, now tight over her swollen child belly, arms slid around her, lightly caressing the gentle curve of her stomach; arms scarred and marked by war, and their owner nuzzled her neck. With a giggle she spun and kissed him, her lips softly touching the scars on his face. "Enough of that, you need to get ready. There will be plenty of time after..."

Zander sighed, pulling his robes from the chest. "I never thought to wear these again," he murmured, as she helped him dress. He was still weak, such wounds as his left a man with lasting souvenirs and he clutched the dark crystal-topped sword cane she had brought him, the stone a match to his locket. Heartstone, it was called.

"Is Peter coming?" he asked, inquiring of the paralysed soldier who had tended him so faithfully when others had not. The young soldier was devoted to his lord, having thrown himself on the Duke's unconscious body to save him.

"He'll be there. This is for him too. I hear he does well enough and he is honoured at court," Eleanor said as she smoothed the red and black robes over his too-thin shoulders and tied the floor-length crimson and black cloak edged with gold. Finally, she fetched the golden crowns, items ancient and powerful in their magic, and giggled as he bent his head to her to receive it and settled hers on her tresses, winding one in his fingers and placing it on his lips.

The walk from the keep to the gardens took far longer than it would for a hale man, but Duke Zander had insisted he would walk to the memorial. It did him good to get the exercise and be seen.

Townsfolk stopped to watch as he passed, some bowed their heads in respect and some threw flowers. This was both a celebration of life and a remembrance of death. There was barely a family who had not been touched in some way by the war. Most of those who had once camped at the walls, those forgotten or ignored by the Council, had returned to their own lands, but a few remained. A dark-haired woman with a small babe in her arms thrust a rose into Eleanor's hand, and Etelka dropped into a curtsy. They had nothing to return to and so they'd stayed and made a new life, and despite the odds, the boy-child thrived. They moved among the crowd to be lost to sight.

A large black stone rose in the centre of the garden, plain and polished to a mirror shine. The musicians played a song of war, a song of hope and finally a song of peace and, with some difficulty, Zander knelt to set the flowers they had bought and those handed to him by the Council members that were clustered around him.

"This day is a day of sorrow, for we must remember those who fell. There are many who lay in a foreign field, who gave their lives in a cause they barely understood. I commemorate this stone, as those in the old days remembered the dead, to them. This day is also a day of joy, for war is over and families are reunited. This day I name 'Eleanor's Day,' for it was she who brought me back, and she who persuaded the Council to agree to peace. It was she who showed kindness to a crippled soldier and his dying friend."

He turned to a face in the crowd, a young man, now in the colours of the city but settled on a small cart. "My friend Peter, a poor man whose bravery was so much greater than many on that field of war, I name freeman of the town and grant him lands in the eastern quarter as Earl of Marchfield."

Bowing his head, Peter muttered he was simply doing his duty. A hand slipped onto his shoulder and the dark-haired widow smiled at him. With a grin, he kissed her hand. There would be no need for a dowry now. Etelka beamed. Her grandson would grow up in a noble house.

As the music began once more, Zander slid his arms about his wife and managed to lead the dancing, until she made their excuses and settled beneath a canopy of red and black to watch the festivities. Gavin and Lynette danced to a very lively jig in the centre of the throng. As the music came to a close, Gavin grabbed her under the arms and scooped her up, swinging Lynette in a wide circle before pulling her in for a passionate kiss.

Eleanor leaned against Zander, watching the strain of the day so far on him, Zander slipped a flower into her hair and whispered something. "Well, I see you are feeling better!" she replied, trying not to laugh.

Dark Lies

Inge-Lise Goss

Piercing sounds of creaking metal, snapping wood and a dull crunching thud startled me into slamming on the brakes. The car jerked to a stop and I gasped. *Damn it!* While keeping my eyes on the garage doorframe, trying not to scrape the side mirror again, I had probably done much more damage.

A stained blue tarp, which had provided a protective cover for Tim's special storage cabinet, now splayed over the front bumper, poking out in different directions.

Throwing the car into reverse, I inched backwards, turned off the engine and closed my eyes in silent prayer. *Please, God, don't let the cabinet be destroyed.* I slid out to survey the damage. I gently lifted the tarp to find the edge of the front car bumper only slightly dented and scratched. Breathing a sigh of relief for that lucky break, I forced myself to yank off the rest of the tarp. *Guess I prayed too late.* Wood chips were scattered all over the floor along with more loose papers than I could count. Dozens of file folders covered the oil-stained concrete, sticking out between slivers of cracked wood. I had demolished the cabinet that held medical research archives, the only remnants Tim had saved from his father's estate. Since they were both doctors who worked on various projects together, these documents were my husband's most precious link to his father.

Tim had ordered a new cabinet to fit into his den, where he planned to move the cabinet's contents. *If only it had arrived before he left for the convention, as the dealer had promised. There's nothing I can do about it now.*

Almost paralyzed, gazing at the destruction in front of me, I regained control when Betsy yelled from the back seat. "Mommy...Bobby waitin'."

"We'll go to the park as soon as I put away the groceries." After unloading the car, I lifted my two-year-old daughter from her car seat and placed her into the stroller.

I calmed myself as we walked the few blocks to the park, my mood warming as I saw my sister Sally's wild, curly auburn hair, so different from my straight hair, a dark brown that almost looked black. Once out of her stroller, Betsy ran off to play with her red-headed cousin Bobby, who was a year older than her, in the sand pile.

I sat down on the bench next to Sally and stared at the children.

"What's wrong?" Sally never missed a signal.

"I hit Tim's father's cabinet when I drove into the garage."

"Wow. Bobby lifted the tarp once and Tim yelled at him. I'd never seen him do that before. What's so special about those old papers anyway? Did they fly in all directions?"

"Some file folders were sticking out between broken wood slats and lots of papers fell out of them, but I didn't see anything that was torn."

Sally patted my arm, her green eyes sparkling. "Just clean it up before he gets home."

"It's just that I feel guilty. Tim was so protective of that cabinet. He even had an extra lock installed to make sure all the contents were secure before he left for the convention. And I wrecked it. The new cabinet came yesterday. If only..."

Sally interrupted. "No problem. Move the files into the new cabinet. Case closed."

"The way he acted about those files, I'm worried about touching any of the papers. But I can't leave them like that in the garage until he gets home. I'll move them tonight."

* * *

After the kids were tired of the park, we took them to the ice cream parlor for a treat.   As we were leaving, we ran into Phil. *My heart jumps every time I see him. Why?* According to Sally, I had been engaged to Phil before the devastating car crash eight years earlier that had killed our parents, put me in the hospital for over two months, and destroyed all my memories. Photo albums were all I had to remind me of life before I was twenty-one. Phil, a good-looking man with a well-built muscular body, still resembled the pictures in the album.

"Hi, Lynne." He nodded to my sister. "Sally." His eyes briefly fixed on mine. The ice cream parlor was among the stores on the first floor of the building owned by Phil's father. Phil's law office occupied the top floor.

Phil bent down and looked at the kids. "How did you two enjoy your ice cream?"

"Liked it, but wanted more whipped cream," Bobby replied.

"Betsy, did you like your ice cream?" Phil asked, leaning closer to her stroller.

Her head bobbed up and down. "Uh-huh. Wanna have it every day."

I shook my head. "Kids."

"Are you going to the town carnival on Saturday?" Phil asked.

"Yes, we'll all be there," Sally said. "The kids wouldn't let us miss it."

"See you then." Phil turned and walked into the building.

"He's the nicest guy." Although she never said so anymore, Sally would've preferred Phil as a brother-in-law.

"I need to get home before Greg gets out of school," I said.

Sally, my only sibling, hadn't been in the car when the accident happened. She was four years younger than me and my rock. Phil's Army reserve status had caused him to be on active duty in Afghanistan when the accident happened. Letters from him didn't mean much to me because I couldn't remember him, or anyone, even Sally.

Tim's father, my neurologist, had trained in New York to specialize in head injuries, but wanted to return to small-town living. Everyone in the hospital kept telling me how lucky I was to have him overseeing my care. One day, while he was testing my memory, Tim came into the room to ask his father something. He smiled at me and said we'd known each other since junior high.

After that, Tim visited me every day. By the time I left the hospital, I was in love with him. We were married before Phil returned home.

I loved Tim, but whenever I saw Phil my heart fluttered and a tingling sensation spread through my body. I always had to resist a compelling desire to wrap my arms around him. Clearly, chemistry or emotion had survived the crash, even if my memories had evaporated.

Because Bradford was a small town, I ran into Phil often. He always gave me a big smile, but I sensed sorrow in his eyes. Phil had never married. I wished he'd find someone who could make him happy and fill the void I must have left in his heart.

* * *

After dinner, I headed to the garage to move the files to the den while Greg, my six-year-old, played with Betsy. Even though the cabinet was badly damaged, I couldn't force the drawers open without the aid of a crowbar. While I carried the last stack of files into Tim's den, he called.

Whenever he was away, Tim called to talk to the kids before they went to bed. I listened anxiously, hoping Betsy didn't mention the cabinet. I felt relieved when she handed the phone to Greg. While they talked, I put Betsy to bed.

As I stepped out of her bedroom, Greg came running down the hallway. "Dad wants to talk to you." Greg frowned. "He got mad as soon as I told him you were putting his files away. I thought he'd be happy."

I gave Greg a hug. "That's okay. He probably wanted to go through them first."

"But he sounded real mad. I've never heard Dad that mad before."

I stroked his cheek. "Don't worry. He isn't mad at you. Why don't you get ready for bed while I talk to him?"

"Okay." Greg headed down the hall.

I went into the living room and picked up the phone. "Hi." I tried to sound upbeat.

"Lynne," he snapped, "Wh–"

"I'm sorry you had to wait so long. I was saying goodnight to Betsy. How's the convention going?"

"Why were you in my father's files?" It was almost a hiss.

"Well...this morning...I accidentally hit the cabinet with my car. It was damaged—not the car—the cabinet. The car only has a little dent in the front bumper. It doesn't need to be fixed."

"Why didn't you just leave the files alone? You know how important they are to me."

"The garage floor is so dirty, papers were strewn everywhere, and I didn't want to leave the documents unprotected. Since the new cabinet's here, I thought the files would be safer in it."

"You should've called me."

"Tim, I'm sorry."

"Are all the files in the new cabinet?"

"No, but they're all in the den. Do you want me to finish putting them away?"

"No. Don't touch them again. I'll be home tomorrow morning and finish the job."

"But the convention won't be over."

"This is more important." He raised his voice in anger. "Make sure the den door stays shut."

"Okay, okay." My hands trembled as I held the phone. Tim had never shouted at me before.

He hung up without saying goodbye.

Staring at the receiver, I lowered it into its cradle. Tim hadn't said "I love you," like he always did. My eyes teared up. I figured he'd be upset, but I hadn't expected that much rage. Dabbing my eyes, I slowly made my way to Greg's bedroom.

"Is Dad still mad?" Greg asked, sitting up in his bed.

"No. He was just worried about Grandpa's papers."

Greg smiled as I kissed him goodnight.

Despite Tim's instructions, I wanted the files to look orderly. In the den, I moved piles from the floor, neatly stacking them on Tim's desk.

When I picked up the last bunch, I noticed my name—my maiden name—on several of the folders. *Why are my files here?* Curious, I took them out to the kitchen table.

I turned on the tea kettle and sat down. Opening the first folder, I found a summary of my condition. Most folders had white labels, but one label was orange. All the sheets inside consisted of formulas. I was startled when the tea kettle whistled. I turned the burner off and came back to read more.

The orange-tabbed file with formulas had notes in the margins. I found "memory" and numbers written on nearly every page, and at the end, "everything learned and taught will remain." Sally had said that my personality hadn't changed as a result of the accident. Uncle Ralph and Aunt Mildred, who'd taken us in, agreed.

I flipped open the third file. The pages were covered with handwritten notes. Tim's dad, like so many doctors, had poor penmanship. I had to concentrate on every word. The first page noted a series of experiments. *Did he need to try something new because my head injury was so severe?*

Next were comments about Tim's dad's research to wipe out memory—to eliminate bad memories that crippled people so they had a hard time dealing with life. He had developed a formula to erase *explicit-episodic memory.* That term was foreign to me, but had to be the purpose of his experiments on me. Tim's handwriting was there, too, with notations on dosages. The last page summarized how many times I had been given the experimental drug along with my reactions and changes in physical and mental condition over the weeks I was being treated.

Horror drifted through me. *Tim's dad stole my memories, and Tim helped him.* I had trusted both of them. He mourned his father when he died. I never mourned my parents because memories about them didn't exist in my mind.

Sally told me that I recognized her when I first woke up in the hospital. But the next day, she said I didn't know her or anyone else. For eight years, I had been clinging to the hope that someday I'd wake up and remember my old life. Now I knew that would never happen. My memories were gone forever.

Grief and dread rolled over me as I returned to the den and neatly placed the folders in plain sight on top of a stack in the center of Tim's desk. I wanted him to know that I knew. Then, somehow, I managed to shower and climb under the covers.

Lying in bed, I stared at the ceiling and thought about the man I had loved for eight years. Tim was a wonderful father, always playing with the kids. He coached Greg's soccer team. The kids adored him. He had taken me on numerous romantic getaways. He even made all the arrangements with either his sister, Alice, or mine to watch the kids. Tim never forgot special occasions. I had been happy with him. *But now—what am I going to do?* I talked to Sally about everything, but how could I tell her or anyone about this? I tossed and turned as tears flowed. *Why had he done this to me?*

* * *

The alarm clock buzzed.

As I opened my eyes, a sharp pain ran through my head. With my hand pressed against my forehead, I dragged myself into the bathroom. A red face and puffy eyes stared back at me in the mirror.

After I cleaned up, I woke up Greg, making sure he didn't see my face.

Hiding it only lasted until Betsy came bouncing into the kitchen. "Mommy, your face!"

I knelt to give her a morning hug. "I think I have a cold. My eyes have been running all night."

"Daddy make ya better."

I smiled at my precious daughter. "I'm sure he will."

When Greg headed off to school, I called Sally and asked her if she could watch Betsy. I told her I wasn't feeling well.

Within twenty minutes she was at the front door. "You look terrible. It's too bad Tim won't be home until tomorrow. You could use a doctor."

"He's coming home today."

As she tucked a strand of loose hair behind my ear, I knew I had to tell her the truth. "Oh, Sally." Tears filled my eyes.

She wrapped her arms around me. "What is it?"

"Tim's dad's experiment," I mumbled. "It was me! I was just an unknowing guinea pig."

Sally's eyes narrowed. "What? What kind of experiment?"

I diverted my eyes toward Betsy playing near the kitchen door, so Sally would understand that I didn't want my child to hear anything bad about her father. "I'm not up to talking about it yet."

"I hate leaving you like this. I could stay here until Tim gets home."

"No, it's better if Betsy goes to your house."

"Try to lie down and get some rest. We'll figure this out together." She hugged me again.

"I can always rely on you. Please, don't mention this to *anyone*, not even Tim."

Sally ran her thumb and index finger across her mouth as if she were zipping it up. "My lips are sealed. Will Tim be home before Greg's out of school?"

I nodded.

"Good. Call me when you're ready to talk." She took Betsy's hand and went to her car.

Drinking a cup of tea, I mulled over my life with Tim-it was all I knew. *Could I leave him and start over again?* My eyes drifted around the room. I couldn't think what to do while I stayed in this house, my dream house that we had designed together. I needed to be alone and away from here to decide what to do. I couldn't bear to stay, letting the children see sadness behind my smiles. All happiness had been drained away.

While I packed a suitcase, the front door opened. "Tim, is that you?" I yelled from the bedroom.

"Yes," he replied, his footsteps pounding down the hallway.

My eyes fixed on the bedroom doorway, expecting him to appear. Instead, the sound of another door being opened and slammed shut echoed through the house. He had gone straight into his den. I closed my suitcase, filled with enough clothes to last a week. I didn't want to be away from the kids longer than that.

I hauled it into the entry hall. As I lowered it to the floor, he came out of the den and headed toward me. He stood silently in front of me and gazed at my face.

Feeling frozen in place, I couldn't budge.

Finally he broke the ice and asked, "Where's Betsy?"

"At Sally's."

"Did you tell Sally about my father's research?"

I lied. "No."

"I told you to leave the files alone," he said angrily. "But you had to snoop."

"Tim, finding out about myself isn't snooping. How could you have done it?"

He stretched out his arms to put them around me.

I backed away. "I'm not ready for your affection. I don't know if I ever will be again."

"Lynne, I have loved you since the first time I saw you. You wouldn't even talk to me, except to say a few words. You're the only one I've ever wanted. Have I been that bad of a husband that you were going to leave without even talking to me about it?"

"You've been a wonderful husband. And father. That's what makes this so hard. I intended to talk to you before I left. But nothing you can say is going to change what happened to me. Your father stole all my memories...completely wiped them out...and you knew what he was doing. If you really loved me, you'd never have allowed that to happen. I wasn't a lab rat for your father to test his theories." My vision clouded. "I'm a human being who had memories—precious memories." I was beyond tears now. "Every year, I put flowers on my parents' grave, though they're just strangers to me. I feel disabled. And it's your fault!" Anger was building up in me. Tim attempted again to wrap me in his arms

"No!" I stood my ground. "I feel lost. You're part of all the memories I have. And now, I don't even know you. You're not the man I thought I married. I don't have a clue what I'm going to do. I need to try and figure it out. But I'll never feel the same way about you."

I saw the pain in his eyes as they focused on me.

"Where will you go?"

"Don't know. I'll drive until it gets dark and find a motel."

"I don't think you should be driving when you're so upset. Why don't you lie down for a couple of hours before you leave?" He paused. "Don't worry, I'll leave you alone. Lynne, as hard as it is for you to believe right now, I have always loved you and I don't want to lose you. You and the kids are everything to me."

I had to admit that I was probably too upset to be behind a steering wheel. I didn't want the kids to be raised without a mother. "I'll try to rest for a little while before I leave."

Once in our bedroom, alone, I took off my shoes, stretched out on the bed. *Could I ever forgive him?* A surge of pain hit me; fear ran through my mind as I thought of living without him. Being his wife was the only life I knew.

I awoke with a start. The clock on the nightstand said 2:53 p.m. Greg would be home soon. I didn't want to see him before I left since I couldn't explain why I was leaving. I slipped on my shoes and hurried down the hall.

Tim sat on the living room sofa, reading the newspaper. He stood up when I entered the room.

Trying to calm my nerves, I took a deep breath. "I need to leave before Greg gets home. You'll have to think of something to tell him and everyone else why I'll be gone for a week."

"Relax. I've already called Sally. She's going to pick up Greg at school. I told her I needed to catch up on some work and I'd get the kids later. Why don't you have something to eat before you go?"

"I'll make a sandwich and eat it while I'm driving." I went into the kitchen with Tim right behind me.

He sat down at the table, and I sensed his eyes on me while I gathered the ingredients. He had watched me often in the kitchen, but now I felt awkward and wished he had stayed in the living room.

"It might be better if you left in the morning," he suggested. "Then you'd have more hours of daylight driving."

"No. I'm leaving as soon as I finish making this."

"Lynne, are you sure this is the right thing to do? Can't you stay so we can try and work this out together? I can't undo the past."

Feeling my throat tightening, I poured a glass of apple juice and took a sip. "No. I want to be alone to decide what to do. I'm only going to be gone a week. Maybe I'll be home sooner. I don't know. Have you figured out what you can tell the kids and Sally?" *I'll call Sally and tell her everything after I check into a motel.*

"I'll say that you're having a severe allergic reaction to something so you're having tests done at the Mayo Clinic in Rochester. How does that sound?"

"Good. That sounds convincing." I took another swig of the apple juice. "This doesn't taste right." I checked the date on the juice container. It hadn't expired, but I still poured the rest of it down the drain.

"I wish you'd stay here," he said. "You could be alone. I could have Alice watch the kids if Sally can't. I'd stay at the hospital. I just don't like the idea of you being on the road by yourself."

"I'll be fine, and I don't like the idea of the kids' routines being any more messed up than necessary. Betsy's toys are here, and Greg's best friend lives next door. You'll have to get someone to watch them here when you go to work."

A look of despair in Tim's eyes engulfed his whole face. It was the same look he had the night his father died. His shoulders slumped. I wanted to comfort him, but stopped myself.

Picking up my suitcase, I headed toward the front door. Halfway there, the room began to sway, and I sank down on the couch. *This emotional upheaval must be taking a toll on me.* I cupped my head in my hands, hoping the dizziness would pass.

"Are you okay?" His voice sounded far away.

"I feel a little dizzy. Just give me a minute."

He sat next to me and put his arm around my shoulders. I lacked the strength to object. My head fell against his chest. Everything went black.

* * *

I slowly opened my eyes and saw a nurse adjusting a tube attached to a needle in my arm. I glanced around the well-equipped hospital room. *Where am I? What happened?*

A tall man dressed in a white lab coat, probably a doctor, stood outside the door, talking to a woman with curly auburn hair.

"Doctor Carlisle, she's awake." The nurse left.

The auburn-haired woman smiled at me as she and the doctor came toward my bed.

The doctor bent down and kissed my lips. "How are you feeling, sweetheart?"

"Do I know you?" I replied, gazing at both of them.

Shock widened the woman's shamrock green eyes. "Not again!"

The Letter

Sean Poage

Arles, France
468 A.D.

Two men sharing a bench outside a taberna would hardly draw a second glance, even in these suspicious times. The throngs of shoppers and the clamour of peddlers made it difficult for anyone to listen in. But the elderly man on the left made such an obvious—and flawed—attempt to blend in with the locals that it only made his pale skin and manicured nails stand out all the more.

The man on the right, a swarthy fellow from the far eastern reaches of the empire, tore a bite out of his moretum-slathered flatbread. From the corner of his eye, he watched the dainty approach the other took to his slice. He puffed a short sigh of exasperation and swallowed. His companion noted the expression and frowned.

"Why, exactly, am I here?" the pale man murmured, just loud enough to be heard through the commotion of the forum.

"My patron understands the difficulties your associates have with the Praetorian Prefect of Gaul. He said you, a famed former holder of that office, would be the one to approach."

"Whatever difficulties we may have, I fail to see why you come to me, or why your patron is concerned."

"Because the Prefect is damaging his interests as well. He sent me to offer a solution."

"What are these interests we have in common?"

"You are aware that Arvandus has cultivated close ties with the court of the Visigoths." The pale man nodded his reply. "We have learned that he has acted treasonously, supplying their king, Euric, with information about military operations planned by Anthemius and his allies."

"You have proof?"

"Nothing you could take to Rome. But my patron has resources in place that can obtain proof, providing it is worth risking his asset to do so."

"So it comes to the purse," the pale man replied, disdain and doubt evident in the curl of his lip. "What is his price?"

"You misunderstand. It is not a reward that my patron seeks. Rather, he looks for the courage to see justice done."

"Nothing more than justice? Few people offer something of value without thought of gain."

"His countrymen work towards the same goals as Anthemius. It would serve his interests to remove a threat to their success."

"To indict one of such high rank is very dangerous."

"Justice requires courage, both of which your record demonstrates. Thus, he had me seek you out."

"I am a politician, not a soldier. This sort of courage would require irrefutable proof; otherwise, it should be called folly."

"What you do with the evidence would rest on your judgement of its worth."

"Your resource is capable of such a dangerous undertaking?"

"Our resource is as skilled and courageous as may be found anywhere in the empire."

* * *

The afternoon sun was high enough to shine directly into the narrow courtyard, illuminating the garden and making the fountains sparkle. Struthe had never set foot in the palace gardens, but she had found this little crevice on the roof of the storerooms where she could look down the slope of the peristyle and admire the view. Having only begun her fourteenth year, she was still thin enough to tuck in and be virtually unnoticeable.

She regarded the piece of wood she held, then licked the tip of her finger and swept it across a charcoal line, smearing it into a hazy cloud over a landscape of trees and fields. She added a few strokes with a charcoal chip and paused to consider her work, chin on hand. Art was her one joy. It even provided a little extra money at the forum. With better materials, she could do so much more, but paint was unattainably expensive. Luckily, she had made a friend who liked her art, and said he would bring her some paint from distant markets.

A mild commotion and the clear ring of a bell floated above the rooftops, announcing the arrival of important visitors. Struthe sighed for the loss of her small free time, paused to gaze out across the expanse of clay-tiled roofs to the sparkling blue-grey curl of the Rodanus, then gathered her things and picked her way back to the little window into the servants' quarters.

The palace received many visitors, expected and otherwise. As Praetorian Prefect of Gaul, Arvandus was powerful and influential, even if the greater part of the lands he governed were, by now, Roman in name only.

The palace complex was managed by a host of servants, some free, most slaves. Struthe's family were freeborn, but among the poor, where jobs were hard to come by, a worker was nearly as chained to his employer as any slave, and trades were often passed down through generations. Her great-great-grandfather had won the post of chief carpenter when the Prefecture moved from Treveris to Arelate, and her father had assumed the post when her grandfather retired. Tragedy struck when her father died three years ago from fever and horrible spasms after stepping on a nail.

Struthe's older brothers had joined the Roman navy before her father died. With no family member to take over his position, her mother, Theophania, feared they would be turned out and left destitute. Luckily, the steward had convinced Arvandus to let Theophania continue on as a menial. Struthe helped by splitting her time between the nursery for the few other small children, including her brother, and other tasks, such as cleaning or running errands. It was enough to get them by.

She put away her materials, then dashed down to the courtyard. She and the other youngsters stood well back, while the adults lined up at the edge of the portico, awaiting their instructions. Her mother glanced over her shoulder, giving a relieved smile to see Struthe there.

In the courtyard, the steward welcomed a delegation of tall, yellow-haired foreigners. Germanic barbarians were not unusual guests here, but some were more important than others. She had to learn where these came from.

While the steward handled the preliminary greetings, the servants received their assignments and scurried off to prepare the guest quarters, stable the horses and put away the baggage. Struthe followed her mother, to help prepare the rooms.

"Who are they?" she whispered.

"Barbarians," her mother replied over her shoulder. "An emissary from the king of the Visigoths. Be very careful! The last time this one was here, Maurus accidentally spilt the envoy's wine and the Prefect sentenced him to twenty lashes." Struthe shivered, remembering the incident. Some whispered that the unnecessary punishment was for nothing more than to impress the Visigoths.

Her mother handed her some bedding and sent her off to prepare one of the rooms. Several of these Visigoths were quartered in the Prefect's private wing, indicating their importance. Struthe hurried through her tasks, then popped out of the room as she heard the boisterous, booming speech of the visitors approaching. She pressed back against the wall and bowed her head as several walked by, led by one of the older servants. None even glanced at her, but going unnoticed suited her. With a sigh of relief, she hurried on to find her next task.

The servants were busy making the delegation at home and preparing a banquet for the evening. Struthe volunteered to help the kitchen staff, running back and forth from the storehouses or fetching water.

Late in the afternoon, the Prefect called for refreshments at his study, where he was receiving the Visigoth envoy. Several of the servants collected platters of food and jugs of wine, then lined up to march down the corridor. Struthe grabbed a basket of bread and joined the line, ignoring the puzzled, condescending look of the older girl in front of her.

Typically, the more mature, developed girls served important guests. The steward appeared in the hall, made a quick appraisal of the group, and with a pair of sharp claps, led them toward the Prefect's chambers.

The wing that housed the Prefect's private rooms was designed like a standard domus, though on a grander, more opulent scale. The tablinum overlooked the atrium, providing a relaxing study for the Prefect to work or entertain favoured guests. Arvandus lounged on a couch, resting a glass on his ample belly and speaking to one of the visitors, a young fellow in rich clothing and a haughty tilt to his head. His guest looked bored but perked up as the servants swept in with food and drink. They quickly laid out everything, executing a sort of dance around the space to avoid stepping between Arvandus and his guest.

Struthe arranged various pieces of bread on a platter, looking at the two men from the corner of her eye. They paid no attention to her, or the other servants. As she finished, the eyes of the Prefect passed over her. Her breath caught in her throat, but his gaze did not linger, and he continued small talk with the young man. Feeling an odd mixture of relief and indignation, Struthe picked up her basket and joined the line of servants as they flowed out through a small door to the narrow passageway that kept the domestics out of view.

She returned her basket to the kitchen and darted off before she could be assigned a new chore. She had a much more important task to accomplish. From the moment she picked up the breadbasket, she had been mulling over how to do so discretely. With an idea formed, she raced to the cellar storerooms to collect a jar of the low-grade olive oil used for lighting, a wooden ladle, and a small terracotta lamp. These went into a basket with a satchel of sawdust and another of sand. Grabbing a stool, she hurried back down the servants' passageway, pausing to duck into an alcove after passing a few other workers.

Struthe took out the lamp and examined it. The red, unglazed clay depicted a pair of women getting water from a well. It was used but had no chips or cracks common to these vessels. She would have to fix that.

Pausing for a moment to listen for anyone approaching, she gave the lamp a sharp tap on the stone corner of the hall, then examined her work. Nothing more than a chip in the clay. She held her breath and gave it another, slightly sharper rap on the marble corner. She let out her breath. She had managed to crack the lamp without breaking it. She filled it with some oil, then put it back into her basket and stood up. Taking a deep breath, she stepped out into the hall and hurried along until she found the correct door.

It opened to a wide hallway behind the tablinum. Doors were spaced along the left, with oil lamps set in iron rings high in the tall marble walls. A courtier, nose high in the air to avoid seeing the menial, passed Struthe as she started down the corridor. She hoped there would not be others, but a thin, elderly man followed a young slave boy out of one of the rooms ahead. She choked and nearly turned back, but they turned away from her and walked down the hall. She exhaled and continued on, well behind them.

At an intersection in the hallway, they turned right, towards the tablinum. When Struthe came to that corner, she paused, her eyes drawn to the left. The corridor continued to a great arch opening to a shaded garden. The late sun glowed on the tips of the trees. To her right, a short vestibule and half a dozen steps rose to the wide entry into the tablinum. The airflow from the atrium to the garden created a cooling breeze through the Prefect's chamber, and the unguarded speech of the occupants carried clearly into the hall.

"Oh, he is nobody. Just my secretary," she heard Arvandus say. "I wish to dictate a letter to your uncle."

Struthe set the basket and stool down against the wall near the corner, then climbed up, stretching to reach the lamp in the hook above.

The Visigoth mumbled an incomprehensible reply in his strange accent.

"Of course, Tulga. Euric knows I have the greatest respect for him," Arvandus said. "That is why I immediately alerted him to their designs when I learned of them last year."

Her heart pounded, and her hands shook as she squatted at the corner. Tulga must be the envoy's name. This must be the sort of information her friend needed. She blew out the wick and poured a little of the oil onto the floor beneath where it had hung.

"A man in my position is a good friend to have," Arvandus continued. "I am the Praetorian Prefect, answerable only to the Emperor. I know of Anthemius's plans almost before he does." Arvandus laughed, his guest responding with a dull chuckle.

"Here, have some more wine, while I describe the latest plots against Euric that scheming Greek is concocting," Arvandus sneered. The disdainful way he said 'Greek' made Struthe grit her teeth. She was Greek, descended from the Hellenes who colonised this region when the Romans still lived in mud huts. Moreover, Anthemius was a popular, just emperor who deserved respect as well as loyalty.

Her resolve steeled, she spat into her palm and mixed in a little sand, using it to scrub the soot off the lamp.

"As I told Euric already," Arvandus continued with a pompous flair, "Anthemius has made a pact with the king of the Britons."

Tulga's low murmur responded while Struthe ladled oil into the lamp.

"He lacks the resources to enforce his will otherwise," Arvandus said. "Even if such belligerence was warranted, it is a poor use of the treasury to waste on such lowly mercenaries."

She moved the stool to another lamp and reached up to light hers. Arvandus's voice was muffled. Moving back to the corner, she used the lamp's flame to light the wick of the broken lamp.

"Despite this, it is evident," she heard Arvandus clearly again, droning in the manner of someone dictating to a scribe, "that the olive branch is thus offered with the one hand, whilst a dagger is concealed in the other."

Once the wick in the broken lamp no longer looked fresh, Struthe blew it out and used the flame from the good lamp to blacken the clay of the broken one.

"While Anthemius's envoys fill your ears with pretences of reconciliation and cooperation, his pawns gather to strike against you."

Satisfied that the broken lamp looked well used, she put it back in her basket.

"It is therefore plain that any thought of making peace with the Greek emperor would be folly. In fact, the law of nations declares that such treachery violates the sacred contract between the Foederatus and the State. The only remedy is to cast aside the threadbare mantle of jilted loyalty."

She moved the stool back and climbed up to put the original lamp back in its holder, breathing a sigh of relief.

"If the Greek emperor will not honour ancient oaths of friendship and confederacy," Arvandus's voice grew bolder, "then a worthy leader would find it his duty to preserve Roman law and tradition against the destructive foolishness of a tyrant. Gaul has long been protected by the effort of the Visigoths and the Burgundians. Reason and the law of nations requires that this be recognised, that there be an end to the long pretence that Rome governs Gaul, and that the sovereignty of Visigoths and Burgundians be acknowledged in their respective realms."

Struthe sprinkled some sawdust and sand on the little puddle of oil, then knelt beside it, poised with a cloth to begin scrubbing if anyone approached.

"But peace is only possible if Anthemius does not have the means to wage war. The most expeditious approach would be to confront and destroy the army of the Britons assembling north of the River Leger. Without the Britons, Syagrius can scarcely defend his own borders much less expand beyond them, and controlling the land the Britons inhabit in western Armorica would strengthen your position in Gaul."

Her timing was perfect, as an elaborately dressed couple, high-ranking members of the court, entered the hall from the garden. They strolled along, arm in arm, tittering and speaking in hushed tones as they passed. They ignored Struthe and continued down the hall and around the corner.

Arvandus continued talking, but Struthe was getting nervous. She understood enough to know it was important, but she needed more than hearsay. A sound of shuffling caught her attention, as Arvandus paused in his dictation.

"I seem to be out of clay for the seal," he said. "Boy, fetch some immediately." Seconds later, the boy she had seen earlier skidded around the corner into the hall. He blinked in surprise to see Struthe there, but noted her scrubbing, gave a quick nod and shot off down the hall to one of the rooms.

Struthe wiped up the remaining mess and gathered her basket. Staying any longer would raise suspicion. Walking away, she heard the returning patter of the boy's feet behind her. There was only one way to get what she needed. She had to get that letter.

Stashing the basket and goods, she went back to the kitchen to listen to the gossip as they prepared for the banquet and evening entertainment. Extra wine would be needed, so Struthe was sent to bring more up. Barbarians were notoriously heavy drinkers who did not even dilute their wine with water. As Struthe knew, Arvandus's own moderation tended to slip when he entertained such guests.

The reception was as lavish as any Arvandus threw, with jugglers, musicians, dancing girls and abundant wine. Struthe always tried to work on the serving crew so she could catch bits of the entertainment, but this night she stayed on the fringes of the activity. When the revelry was at its peak, she retrieved her basket and stole away to the personal quarters, a long hall on the second floor.

She stood in the shadows at the servants' stairway, listening for any sound. The hallway was dim, lit with fewer lamps, but the moon shone through the small windows high in the walls. She knew where Tulga would sleep that night. Well, she was reasonably certain. With luck, the letter would be there. Arvandus must have given it to him, and she could not imagine Tulga would take it to the banquet.

As she stood in that darkened nook, considering all the things that could go wrong, she began to shake. If caught, they would kill her. At the very least, her family would be evicted and left destitute. But if she were successful, it would go a long way towards getting them all away from this. From him. She took a deep breath and stepped out into the hall.

She carried the basket and lamp oil again. It would provide an excuse if questioned about being in this area. At the first of the apartments, at the far end of the hall from where she had stood, she paused to listen at the door, then opened it and peeked in. A single lamp provided enough light to prevent tripping and little more. She gulped and stepped in, pushing the door closed behind her, thankful they kept the hinges well oiled.

The rooms seemed unoccupied. When her eyes adjusted, she saw that the sitting room she stood in contained the envoy's baggage, still mostly packed. She picked her way towards the bedchamber, then stopped. On a table against the wall, a rolled-up parchment poked out of a satchel. She pulled it out, realising she had no way to know if it was the letter or not. She could not read. She could think of no other reason for it to be there. It had the metallic tang of fresh ink. Even if she could read, the scroll was secured with string, with a bit of clay molded around the knot and imprinted with a seal. Certainly, Arvandus's seal. The clay was still tacky and fresh. It must be the letter.

But it would be missed. She had brought a parchment she had stashed away for sketching and planned to copy the letters onto it, replacing the envoy's letter afterwards. But that wouldn't be possible without breaking the seal. She needed to get a bit of that clay and Arvandus's seal.

She slipped back out into the hallway and hurried back downstairs to Arvandus's study.

The sound of merrymaking was clear in this part of the palace, and Struthe was grateful that everyone seemed to be attending. She slipped into the tablinum and paused to let her eyes adjust. There were no lamps here, but moonlight sparkled on the pool beneath the atrium's open roof, and it offered enough light to manage.

She poked around at the table beside the couch where Arvandus had lounged. Stacks of parchments, some scrolls and wooden wax tablets, a few dice, a knife and other odd baubles cluttered the surface. In a small wooden box, she found a lump of clay that felt like that of the seal. She pinched off a piece and put it on the table, frustrated that she could not find anything to make the seal's imprint. Footsteps and whispers, followed by a snorting laugh made her heart jump into her throat.

Struthe dropped to the floor and crawled under the table as a pair of shadows stumbled up the steps and into the chamber. They flopped onto the couch with a laugh and slurred exclamations, close enough for Struthe to reach out and touch them. She recognised Arvandus's voice, but the other was a woman she did not know. Perhaps a member of the court, a servant, or a prostitute; it did not matter. They reeked of wine and seemed to have scarcely enough wits about them to communicate in more than grunts and giggles.

She squeezed her eyes shut and clapped her hands over her ears. Their activities were noisy, bestial, flailing. It was over sooner than it seemed, and the two of them sprawled on the couch panting for a few minutes. As their breathing slowed, Arvandus's took on a different tone, and he began to snore. His companion sat up, and after a moment stood with a contemptuous snort and padded out through the atrium.

Struthe sat there, still frozen, certain that he would wake at any moment and discover her, but his snoring continued unabated. She inched out from under the table and crouched behind it. Reaching out to find her lump of clay, her fingers came upon the hilt of the knife and stopped. She slowly stood, her breath short and quick in her chest, the blood beginning to throb in her ears.

Enough light reflected into the room to illuminate the carefully curled and oiled locks framing his pale, fat face. The face that had sneered down at her, terrified her, violated her. She took a step around the table, the knife gripped in her hand the way she had wished she could grip his fleshy neck. Another step and she was standing over him. She stared down at him, recalling his acrid breath in her face, the weight of his bulk pushing her down. What he took from her she could never recover. What decent man would want her, when that time came? She was freeborn, no slave to be treated as property. Where could she find justice? He had made it plain that if she said anything, he would call her a liar, her brother a thief and her mother a whore, before casting them all out to starve on the streets.

The knife hung above him. The world held no justice for one such as this. Perhaps it would find him at the final judgement.

The knifepoint wavered. Would murder be justice in the eyes of God, or would she damn herself? If she were found out, would anyone believe her story, her motive? She remembered the letter, the entire purpose for her being in that room. It might be a sort of justice, and it would not leave blood on her hands that she could never wash away. The pounding in her ears faded and left her trembling. She laid the knife on the table, located the clay and fled the room.

In a quiet corner of the palace, she huddled in a corner to catch her breath and calm her nerves. Was all this worth it? Was she out of her mind to think she could do anything about this man? Was she being selfish to risk her family like this?

"*What could I possibly offer?*" she had asked her friend. "*I'm just a child of a nameless family.*"

"*So many important things happen by people doing small things in their own interest,*" he had replied. "*You are capable of far more than you dare believe.*" She smiled at the inspiring memory.

Arvandus leaving the banquet worried her. Would that signal an end to the night? The sounds of revelry continued, but for how long? She would not have time to copy the letter and return the original.

Struthe pulled the scroll out of the basket and examined it. Hints of writing showed through thin spots in the parchment and along the edges. She unrolled her precious piece of parchment and made random marks across it, approximating the bits of writing she had seen over the years. It would be utter gibberish when opened, but with luck, it would not matter by then.

She rolled the parchment up, ran the string through and around it in the same manner as the original and tied the knot in the same place. She applied the clay in the same manner over the knot and then sat back to compare.

It might do, especially if Tulga was not too interested in the letter. However, it lacked the imprint of Arvandus's seal, and this would not pass unnoticed. She studied the imprint of the seal on the original. It was a simple design, a stick figure holding a vine. She broke a piece of wicker from her basket and used it to carve a reasonable copy of the seal, impressing herself with her work. She had one task left for the night, and she prayed that Tulga had not yet wearied of the dancing girls and wine.

The hallway was empty and quiet. She approached Tulga's door, footsteps scuffed on the stairs and a moment later, two tall blonde Visigoths turned the corner. She nearly fainted, but neither man was Tulga. They passed by and went into one of the other apartments, ignoring the simple servant girl making the rounds of the oil lamps.

Struthe doubled back to Tulga's door and tapped on it. No answer, so she pushed it open. Nothing appeared to have changed since her last visit. Moments later, the fake scroll was in the satchel, and she was back in the hall, hurrying towards the stairs to the servant's corridor, lightheaded with relief.

She went directly to her family quarters, relieved her mother was not there. Her brother would still be with the other youngsters. She would feign illness if sought out, and with the way she felt, it would not require a grand theatrical performance. She hid the scroll and collapsed on her bed.

It was a sleepless night. She fretted and started at every sound, certain that soldiers would burst through their door at any moment. When her mother returned, Struthe claimed illness, so her mother made her drink some herbed wine before going to her own bed.

As usual, the servants rose before the dawn to begin their many duties. Struthe's lack of sleep made her look even worse, so Theophania commanded her to stay in bed for the day before she left to attend to the chores.

By the time the morning sun spread a rosy glow across the sky, Struthe was darting through alleyways to the waterfront, the stolen scroll hidden under her shawl. The fishermen were preparing their boats to cast off and the merchant vessels were loading their wares as she scurried along the street of the docks. She had seen her friend at the market a few days before, though he had furtively waved her off from approaching him. She prayed he was still in the city.

Not seeing him along the wharf, she began to panic, asking around for anyone who might know the whereabouts of a Syrian trader. The sun was up and the wharf was becoming crowded. She turned down an alley that led towards the market and nearly bowled over a dark-skinned elderly fellow who stepped out of a warehouse door.

"Hasdi!" she exclaimed.

"Ah, my young sparrow!" Hasdi smiled at her. "What has you flitting about so?"

"I've brought you something," she gasped, relief and sudden trepidation fighting within her as she worried what the future would bring.

* * *

Author's Note

About 468 CE, the Western Roman Empire was in the final years of its ruin. According to surviving records, the Emperor, Anthemius, made a pact with the "King of the Britons", a man called Riothamus, to help fight against Visigoth expansion in Gaul (France). Any hopes of stemming the Empire's collapse were crushed when Arvandus, the governor of Gaul, revealed Anthemius' plans to Euric, the king of the Visigoths. The content of the letter and the results are recorded in history and legend.

Research by the late, famed historian, Geoffrey Ashe, showed that the origins of the legends of King Arthur are based partially on these events, and that Riothamus, a Latinization of the Brittonic for "Highest King" was actually a title for Arthur.

How the letter that Arvandus sent to Euric was intercepted has been lost to history. This story is an attempt to imagine such an effort, and is a sort of prequel to the historical fiction novel, *The Retreat to Avalon*, the first novel in the series, *The Arthurian Age*, by Sean Poage.

The Book of Ruth

Rebecca Lacy

Life in rural southeast Missouri wasn't always easy. Lord knows, we had seen our share of difficult times. In just a few short years we had lived through a world war, the depression, droughts, and floods. Despite all the upheavals inflicted on the world, I always felt optimistic. I believed my community and my family could overcome any obstacle.

Then, that sense of security was stripped away in an instant one terrible Sunday when war once again intruded on our lives.

December 7th began so innocently. The church was having its annual potluck luncheon to celebrate the hanging of the greens. The dining room in the basement was full of laughter and an air of expectation with Christmas just weeks away. This year, the holiday was like a beacon of light in the darkness as Europe became embroiled in a war that threatened to spill out into the rest of the world.

In the months leading up to that day, it had become increasingly apparent that America would soon be joining the fight. As much as it was the country's policy to remain objective, our allies were pleading for assistance. The question on everyone's lips was 'How long can we remain out of the fray?'.

The answer was delivered to our door during the celebration. It was Charlie Olsen who bore the news, unchecked tears streaming down his face. The tables were crowded with congregants enjoying food and fellowship. Charlie, whose wife, Mary, and their children were seated at the table next to ours, typically found other activities, which prevented him from joining his family for Sunday worship. Everyone knew it was just so he could read the Sunday paper in peace while their five kids were out of the house.

When Charlie burst in, a hush spread through the hall as we became aware that something was wrong. An unsettling quiet descended, and all eyes turned to Charlie. With his voice trembling, he told us what he had heard on the radio: Pearl Harbor had been attacked.

As the news sank in, we were stunned into silence. The only sounds were a quiet sob, and a child's whisper demanding, "What's a Pearl Harbor?" followed a few seconds later with, "Where's Hawaii?"

No doubt there were many in the hall wondering, as I was, what this would mean to our families. I watched my son, Tom, as Charlie recounted the news, and I saw his jaw set and his fists clench. That was all I needed to know my son would want to join the fight.

Pastor Morris gathered us in prayer as we grappled with the mix of emotions I saw written on the faces around the room. He implored us to keep our wits about us, to love one another, and not wait another day to tell those we care about how we feel.

"This goes to show, that life is a treasure we must never take for granted. Today's events will undoubtedly change our world considerably. There are frightening times ahead, but with our loved ones, and God's guidance and mercy, we will get through it," he said.

On the way home, I sat between my husband and Tom in our pick-up truck. On a typical Sunday the three of us would be talking about the service and sharing the gossip we had overheard. Instead, we rode home in silence, each of us lost in our own thoughts.

The way John gripped the steering wheel suggested he was cursing the Japanese for the attack. I suspected he was also blaming the president for not entering the battle sooner. My husband is a man of few words and is as peaceful as any human being I've ever known. However, it had bothered him for some time that the US was allowing bullies to push around the rest of the world.

During a visit to the farm a few days earlier, I overheard his brother, Oscar, say it was none of our business if other countries were getting beat up. John had emphatically responded, "Closing our eyes to what's happening in the world isn't my idea of what being an American is all about,"

When we got home, we sat close to the radio, our heads bent as though by the weight of the news we were listening to. We learned several ships had been hit during the early morning raid, and of those, some had sunk, carrying an unknown number of American men to their deaths. Firsthand accounts told of horrors no one could have escaped, and I wept as I thought about the fear they must have experienced in their final moments, and for the families who had lost so much that day.

We stayed glued to the radio until late in the evening. Even though many of the reports offered nothing new, we continued to listen as though hearing it over and over again would somehow make it more real. Like a child, I listened hoping it was all just radio theatre such as *War of the Worlds*. I knew intellectually that this was not the case, but I wanted it to be. I even caught myself mentally scripting scathing words to send to those who would perpetrate such a cruel joke on an unsuspecting public. Of course, it wasn't a hoax. It was the end of the world as we knew it. Unlike the Orson Wells' play, however, it wasn't at the hands of space aliens. It was the result of man's inhumanity to man.

When we finally went to bed, I tossed and turned as my mind raced. As much as I tried not to worry or think the worst, it was impossible not to see what this was going to mean to our family.

Around 3:00 a.m. I gave up trying to sleep and, I went to sit on the porch. I was wrapped in a quilt made of patches that reminded me of happier times, watching the steam rise off the cup of tea I forgot to drink. Numb with cold and fear, I sat there until the first hint of red rouged the horizon. I wished I could hold off dawn a few more hours.

My wishes to postpone morning were ignored, of course. After all, cows are very self-centered creatures and aren't inclined to give their human caretakers a pass. We all had work to do before the sun crested the horizon.

John and Tom chatted about their day over breakfast. It was a typical conversation I had overheard a thousand times. The words were similar, but there was something different. The air was thick with tension and unspoken thoughts, making it difficult to breathe. After breakfast, they headed for the barn, where, I suspected, they would have the conversation they neatly avoided in my presence.

All day, I seemed to be in a stupor as I baked bread and cleaned the house without really thinking about what I was doing. A radio newscaster kept up a constant monologue about the attack in the background as I worked. He said war was inevitable now - there was no way for the U.S. to remain neutral. It was reported the peace talks with Japan had been a hoax. Apparently, they had been plotting the attack for weeks if not months. Finally, I couldn't bear to hear anymore, and switched off the radio.

Sometime before noon, John turned it back on and the three of us awaited President Roosevelt's address to Congress. John looked haggard, dark circles under his eyes, his hair standing up in cowlicks from running worried fingers through it. My heart ached for him. I had been so preoccupied by my own fears and worries that I had ignored the fact that he too was experiencing similar emotions. Beside him was Tom, with elbows on his knees, chin in his hands, staring at his feet. I sat in my sewing rocker opposite them, with my sweater pulled tight around me, trying to quiet the nerves making me shiver.

As anticipated, the president declared that America would be entering the war. John and Tom sat up a little prouder when he stated, "No matter how long it may take us to overcome this premeditated invasion, the American people in their righteous might will win through to absolute victory."

As I listened to the president, all I could think of was the possibility of losing the people I loved most. There was no victory to be found in that.

When the speech was over, John slowly stood and switched off the radio saying, "Well, that's that."

I reached up to take his hand and he returned the squeeze. I could see he was trying to master his emotions and would have nothing more to say on the matter for the time being.

I went to the kitchen to fix lunch and John quietly let himself out the door, heading to the small room in the barn he used as his refuge. Meanwhile, Tom retreated to his room, closing his door softly behind him.

During the weeks following Pearl Harbor and the declaration of war, Farmington drew closer together. The stores were crowded with shoppers taking time to chat with one another in hushed voices while stocking up on provisions, which everyone predicted would soon be in short supply.

Photographs in the paper showed long lines at recruitment centers where young men signed up to fight for our country. There were even some not-so-young men eager to join the fray.

The pews at church, which were normally only crowded during Christmas and Easter, were overfilled. The ushers set up chairs along the back and in the aisles of the sanctuary to accommodate the visitors. Each of us came looking for a promise of safety and hope. Many who gathered would soon be leaving to join the fight. Others would have family and friends shipping off to foreign lands to face an enemy we knew so little about. How had this happened to us? There were so many questions and we sought answers and comfort from a God who seemed to have grown silent in the hour when we needed Him most.

There were some in town, such as Fred Hickman, who proclaimed they couldn't worship a God who would allow such evil to go unchecked. "How," Fred asked anyone who would listen, "can you worship a being who would allow such monstrous acts. If He exists at all, He is an uncaring bastard."

The harshness of the words shocked me. I grew up believing God gave mankind free will. If we chose to exercise it in a manner that was destructive and murderous, it was on us. Not only did He give us free will, but He gave us the ability to distinguish right from wrong and make decisions based on that. He gave us the ability to think and reason. He gave us the capacity to love and empathize. If, despite those gifts, we still engaged in the wholesale slaughter of one another, then we weren't worthy of our place in the world.

Overall, I trusted my deep-seated convictions. However, sometimes, doubts crept in. During those times, I couldn't help feeling someone needed to be held accountable. Why not God? Surely, he could stop the madness if he wanted to.

There were times when I was in prayer, I expressed my anger at His apparent lack of concern about what was happening to His children. On those occasions, I would flip open my Bible to a random page looking for hope and guidance.

On one occasion, I was seeking answers to questions I found difficult to formulate. I closed my eyes, opened my Bible to a random page, and put my finger down. Opening my eyes, I saw the scripture my finger had landed on was Isaiah 45:7. '*I form light and create darkness, I make well-being and create calamity, I am the Lord, who does all these things.*'

Was this passage telling me I was wrong in thinking God had had nothing to do with this terrible war? Was He really behind this horror? The thought filled me with sorrow and made me feel alone in a very dangerous world.

Surely there was more to this message hidden in the rest of the chapter. I readily admit I'm not a Bible scholar. Even as a child in Sunday school, I had difficulty paying attention to the lessons. In truth, I was only familiar with some of the basic tenants even though I was in church every Sunday. Thus, I didn't really understand what I was reading, but the tone gave me renewed hope. As I understood it, God was angry about those who would attack His children and He would equip them to fight the good fight so they would come out victors. 'I will set my exiles free.'

I didn't know what lay ahead for my family or my country, but I had renewed hope that God would deliver us in the end.

Even though I had hope to cling to, it was, nevertheless, sad and frightening to feel the city growing quieter and more subdued as young men shipped off for basic training. My childhood friend, Lizzie Krieg, had twins who enlisted together leaving their mother proud and scared. Dr. Winters' grandson, Joseph, was one of the first to enlist. A friend of the family reported the doctor was inconsolable when the young man came home from St. Louis, where he was in medical school, to tell his family of his decision. They begged him to reconsider. They assured him he would be better able to help if he completed his education and could serve as a doctor. Their words fell on deaf ears. Like so many others, Joseph felt the call to action.

It wasn't just the families with sons who were affected. Bill and Peg Miller's oldest daughter, Deborah, left to serve as a field nurse, and the Blue's pregnant daughter, Katherine, moved back from Hannibal to stay with her parents after her husband reported for duty. I saw her at Dad's store a few days later. Her lip trembled as she tried to smile and return my greeting. When I reached out to her, she hurried out of the store, forgetting her package.

In those very early days, I continued to be hopeful that Tom would choose to stay and help his dad. Farming would be more important than ever with so much food needed to supply the war effort. In my mind, staying home to support the country in this manner was the patriotic thing to do. After all, one less soldier wouldn't make a difference, but one less farmer certainly would.

I held onto that hope until a blustery night in late January when Spring was still months away. The men came in after the last of their chores and we ate in silence, something that had become a habit since the attack on Pearl Harbor. As I began to clear the dishes, John took my hand in his and asked me to sit down. "Tom and I have something we need to talk with you about."

They both wore the look I had learned to distrust over the years.

Instantly a chill ran up my spine. I didn't want to sit down: if I could just stay busy, they wouldn't be able to tell me anything I didn't want to hear. So, I tried to pull away saying, "The dishes won't wash themselves. Whatever it is can wait until I'm done."

John held on to my hand, giving an almost imperceptible shake of his head. I sank back into my chair, certain of what they needed to tell me.

I stared at them, daring them to speak. Typically, that well-honed look makes them squirm and silences them, but it didn't work on that occasion.

"Mom," Tom said, "I've decided to enlist."

Even though I knew it was coming, his words hit me like a slap in the face.

We sat in silence for what felt like minutes. The only sound was the ticking of the mantel clock.

"Well, say something," Tom pleaded, breaking the silence.

"What should I say?" I asked dully.

"Say, it's okay. Tell me to go to my room. I don't know. Just say something."

"Very well, here it is: Your father and I need you here. The farm isn't going to run itself. There are plenty of other young men who can serve while you are helping to support the effort from right here, where you belong."

"I've thought it all through, Mom, and this is what I need to do."

"That is so selfish, Tom!" I heard my voice getting shrill as my desperation increased. This was not the woman I wanted to be, but he needed to hear me.

"I'm sorry you feel that way. My decision is made. I'm going and I hope you will give me your blessing."

I bit the inside of my mouth and stared at the wall over Tom's shoulder, unwilling to look him in the eye, fighting tears so he wouldn't see how hurt I was...how angry I was...how afraid I was. When he got up and went outside, I remained frozen in my seat.

John hadn't said anything; rather he had kept his hands folded on the table with his head slightly bowed as though in prayer. Finally, he reached over to cover my hand with his, but I jerked away.

"Don't," I commanded. "Don't try to offer me solace when you are responsible for his decision."

For the second time that evening, I saw my words had hit their mark. John's eyes clouded with sorrow, and it gave me a lump in my throat. In the twenty-two years we had been married, there had been very few times when words of discord had passed between us, and I don't think I had ever said anything to him that had cut so deep.

"Ruth, I didn't convince him to go. It was his decision. I don't want him to go any more than you do."

"Maybe you didn't suggest it, but you two have been thick as thieves, hiding out in the barn for the past month. I know you have discussed this. He confided in you and sought your advice just like he's done his whole life."

As I had foreseen the first time John held Tom as a red, wrinkly newborn, they had become inseparable. They adored one another and had grown to be so much alike that at times it felt as though they were the same person at different stages in life. I was certain Tom would never make such a critical decision without seeking advice from his father.

"Of course, he asked me what I thought," he confirmed.

"And what did you say? Did you tell him he needs to stay here?"

"No. I told him he's the only one who can make that decision."

"You told him what? You had the opportunity – no, scratch that – you had the responsibility as his father to persuade him to stay and work the farm. We need him here."

"There's one thing you've forgotten, Ruth: Tom's a man now. It's his decision to make."

"He's still a teenager, for God's sake, John. How can he make a decision like this? What does he know about war?"

"Whether you want to admit it or not, he is a man. Besides, what do any of us know about war? But one thing is certain: we're in a fight for our freedom, and Tom feels he needs to be a part of that. Believe me, Ruth, it wasn't an easy decision for him. He had to weigh the risks and balance that against his conscience..."

"His conscience?" I demanded.

"Yes, of course. His friends and schoolmates are enlisting all around him. If he stays here, nice and safe, it will make us feel better, but what about him? He feels duty-bound to do his part. We didn't go looking for this war, it came looking for us, and Tom feels called to action. Frankly, if they would have me, I would enlist myself, but I'm too old."

As soon as the words were out of his mouth, John knew his mistake. I was shocked. I had never even thought about him wanting to enlist. I tried to speak but couldn't formulate the words.

"Honey, all I'm saying is that when something like this happens, men like Tom and I feel a responsibility to defend our homes, our country. We don't feel right leaving it up to someone else."

I took a deep breath, trying to calm my emotions. I needed to reason with him...make him understand. "You are his father, the person he looks up to more than anyone on earth. You can persuade him if you would try. He will listen to you. You can make him stay home."

"And what? Be a momma's boy? Is that what you want? Is this about protecting him or making you feel better?"

"Both!" I snapped. So much for mastering my emotions.

"He isn't your little boy anymore. You have to let him go and give him your blessings."

"No I don't. I refuse to send him off to war willingly. I will claw and fight to keep him here. He's my only son." My voice was beginning to quiver, but I refused to cry.

"He's my only son, too, you know. It isn't any easier for me than it is for you."

"I don't believe that. Women know the pain of bringing a child into the world only to see them used as a pawn in some monstrous game. It's more than we can bear.' With mounting anger and frustration, I continued. "And yet, here we are again. Another generation forced to fight a war they didn't choose. Men are in charge, just like always. They are the ones who started this war just like they always have. So how can you possibly say it's the same?"

"I didn't start this war."

"Maybe not, but you're willing to sacrifice our son. If Tom dies in this war, it will be your fault."

"How can you say that?"

I was so furious, I couldn't respond.

We sat in an uncomfortable silence for some time before John's chair scrapped the floor as he abruptly pushed back from the table. He went out the door, letting it slam behind him. Undoubtedly, he was going to join Tom in the barn, where the two of them would remain until they thought I was asleep, and it was safe to return to the house.

We never discussed the matter any further. It was pointless. Tom went to the recruiting center the next day and I fixed him his favorite dinner as a peace offering. I didn't back down from my conviction, but there was nothing I could do to alter things at that point. I was thankful they had at least told me before his enlistment, so I had an opportunity to try to change his mind.

Three weeks later, on a frigid February morning, Tom boarded a bus with his two best friends and several other boys from town, all of whom were headed to basic training at Ft. Leonard Wood where they would remain for the next 12 weeks or so. Then his unit would be transferred for advanced infantry training before they were shipped out.

We were joined by about 30 other people to wave them off. During the first wave of recruits to leave, there had been big celebrations – practically ticker-tape parades. Over the weeks, people had grown weary of the departures. What had begun as a rally for patriotism had become less celebratory. The loved ones of those leaving put on a brave face with hearty slaps on the back and jabs in the arm from brothers and fathers, hugs from mothers and sisters and wives carefully holding back tears. For most of these young men, it was the first time they would ever be away from home for more than a few days. Many had never even been out of St. Francois County.

John's mother, May, was there to say goodbye. She had left the farm and moved in with her sister in St. Louis a few years after Tom was born. Even though she was getting on in years, nothing could have kept her from coming to see him off – not even an uncomfortable 75-mile bus ride.

May's demeanor was bright and cheerful, as though he was preparing to go to college instead of war. I envied her sunny optimism until I saw her face when Tom wasn't looking. In those unguarded moments, she looked every bit as worried as I felt. I realized it was the icy wind keeping the tears from streaming down her face. Mother Nature, it would seem, was in on the conspiracy with the women assembled to help us put on a brave face for our loved ones.

When the bus departed, we watched and waved until it was out of sight. John, May, and I drove home in silence. It reminded me of the ride home on the Sunday we heard about the bombing of Pearl Harbor.

Dinner that night was a subdued affair punctuated with a few musings about what Tom and the boys would be doing at that time or what they would have to eat.

After dinner, we gathered in the living room around the fire. May sat on the couch, knitting a scarf she planned to send to Tom while John poked and stirred the fire, his habit when feeling unsettled. I rolled bandages as I did most every night – my small contribution to the war effort. It was quiet, too quiet to feel comfortable.

The silence was broken by May's laugh, an odd mixture of cackle and cough. "Do you remember the time when Tom was just a tyke, and the Fieldings came for lunch? Tom had been down for a nap, and we were gathered around the table. Pastor Fielding was saying grace. Remember? Tom came running in naked as the day he was born, demanding to know why we were having a party without him."

"I remember that!" John exclaimed. "I thought Pastor Fielding was going to die laughing."

"I was mortified," I chimed in. "My first luncheon for the new minister and his wife and my son decides to crash the party in his birthday suit! I just knew they were going to think I was a terrible mother. When he started laughing, I could have kissed him."

"Tom or the pastor?" asked May.

"Both!"

"The real kicker was Mrs. Fielding. Remember what she did? She took her napkin and folded into a diaper and tied it onto him. Remember how tickled Tom was? He made sure that everyone saw his fancy party diaper," May recalled.

I'm certain that somewhere at Ft. Leonard Wood, Tom's ears were burning as we spent the rest of the evening recounting stories about our favorite boy. I chuckled thinking how embarrassed he would be if he knew. The laughter and sweet memories made that first night bearable.

As the months passed tension and uncertainty mounted. Everywhere one went, the news was the primary topic of discussion: What will Hitler's next move be; which country will be the next to fall into enemy hands? We had all become masters of current events and most of us had learned more about world geography than we ever could have imagined possible when we were in school. Those points on the map were no longer foreign places of little interest. Now they were places where our loved ones were being sent to fight and possibly die.

I must admit, despite my deep-seated fears, I was enormously proud of Tom. His letters told of his journey into manhood, and I read each one over and over until his words were etched into my mind. I was relieved that he seemed to be thriving in his new environment.

When Tom finally came home for leave, I was taken aback at the changes I saw in him. He wore a military bearing – a formality – I had never seen in him before. He stood more erect, he spoke with more deference to John and me and other 'adults' he encountered. He moved differently, too – with greater assurance and purpose. Gone was the teenager who needed to be reminded to pick up after himself. That boy had been replaced by a man who needed to be encouraged to let someone else do for him once in a while. His face, always lean, had become almost chiseled, his aquiline nose, a feature inherited from my father, was a bit more prominent. What hadn't changed was his sense of humor. When I hugged him, he picked me up and swung me around, setting me back on my feet with a wicked twinkle in his eyes.

When the day came for him to return to duty, a parade of soldiers ready to deploy marched down Columbia Avenue. The shopkeepers came out to join the throng of people lining the street. Children waved tiny American flags handed out by the Boy Scouts. It was a proud moment for the town. These were our fine young men. They had grown from children into adults with the bearing and strength of warriors.

After the parade, there was just enough time to grab a quick bite before they boarded the bus. That would be the first leg of a journey that would take them far from the safety and comfort of home to a world that was totally foreign. When it came time for them to leave, John and I were joined by a throng of people hugging Tom and pumping his hand with wishes for good luck. Several of the women from church gave him and the other boys wrapped parcels of goodies guaranteed to make their travels a little sweeter.

As they boarded the bus, there was a sense of boyish camp revelry among them. Maybe it was designed to put their loved ones at ease. Or maybe it was a way for them to avoid seeing the fear behind the smiles we all wore.

The house was unnaturally quiet that evening. It's funny how every time Tom came home, he breathed new life into it. Then when he left, the air seemed to leave with him.

Shortly after Tom's deployment, I found John in his office where he was hunched over the books, squinting at the figures he was entering into the narrow columns. I wrapped my arms around him and buried my head on his shoulder and didn't say a word.

I had never apologized for all the terrible things I had said to him the night Tom told me he was going to enlist, and for how cold I was afterwards. I had treated him like an enemy at the very time we needed to come together. The words whirled around in my mind, but nothing came out. Nothing I could say would ever adequately convey my regret or my contrition.

"I know, I know," is all John said as he held me.

After that, I felt a great weight was lifted off me. I had a sense of peace I couldn't quite trust. There were still things I needed to work out with God. "I know You've told me not to worry and to put my trust in You," I prayed. "But You know me, God, that isn't something that's easy for me to do. I know You are with Tom. Please, do your best to keep him safe."

* * *

Over time, it became increasingly difficult to find any farmhands to help out. May came back down from St. Louis so I could spend more time assisting John. We tried not to complain, realizing how much better we had it than so many others.

However, the summer heat was testing our good humor. The sun beat down with unrelenting intensity. After a particularly hot day, John and I were resting on the porch. He had just come in after an arduous day doing the job of three men in the fields. I had tended the animals and worked in the victory garden. We were both beat, looking forward to super and an early bedtime. A slight breeze blew, offering a little relief from the heat as we sat in companionable silence. We sipped sweet tea, and the sweat dripped off the glasses making tiny mud spots where it landed on our soiled clothes.

In the distance, I could see a plume of dust being kicked up by a car heading in our direction. There were only a couple houses beyond ours, so they were either coming to see us, the Millers or Sawyers. We weren't expecting company, and not too many people just dropped in these days with gas rationing in effect. So, I assumed that the vehicle would continue down the road and was surprised when it turned into our drive. When it got closer, the dust cleared, and I saw that it was Melvin Short's blue sedan and my throat constricted in panic.

Mr. Short had been delivering telegrams around Farmington and the outlying area for as long as I could remember. He used to be a welcome sight, for the most part, bringing news of births and weddings as well as the sadder type of messages.

We watched in tense silence as the car made its way to our house. My heart began pounding in my chest and my ears were ringing as blood rushed to my head. Next to me, I heard John say, "Oh, no," in a voice that was nearly inaudible.

Since the war started, the sight of Mr. Short had become as unwelcome as the angel of death himself. No one wanted to see his car pull into their drive. The man had aged by at least a decade in the past year or so. The glint of humor had gone out of his eyes, which were downcast as he walked toward us, shoulders stooped with an unseen burden.

My hands began to shake uncontrollably, and tea glass slipped out of my fingers, shattering on the porch. The sound startled the man, and he halted, waiting for his senses to register what had happened. When he saw the shards of glass, he understood and began moving towards us once more.

I saw the telegram envelop in his hand and I wanted to yell at him to get back in his car and leave us alone. I probably would have if only I could have found my voice. But the only sound to be heard was a distant cardinal's song and Mr. Short's shoes on the walkway.

John stood and took a couple steps towards him. For a moment or two, the tableau froze, no one moving or speaking.

"John, Ruth...I'm sorry to have to give you this," he said, handing my husband the envelop. I moved woodenly so I could read it over his shoulder.

WE REGRET TO INFORM YOU YOUR SON TOMAS J MONROE...

I don't know what else it said because my knees buckled, and I fell to the ground in a weeping heap. John held me as we watch the plume of dust retreat down the road, taking Mr. Short and the last shreds of our happiness.

I'm not certain how long we sat there before John helped me stand. With his arm still around me, he stared with unseeing eyes off into the distance. His face was ashen, his chest rising and falling with labored breath. I wanted to touch him, to offer him comfort, but I couldn't. I was too lost in my own vortex of darkness to reach out beyond it to connect with him.

After a few minutes holding one another, John kissed the top of my head and said, "I've got to go make sure everything is in order in the barn. Don't wait supper for me." As he walked away, I noted his normally erect posture now mirrored that of Mr. Short.

The following week I drove to church alone. John, who had almost never missed a Sunday, begged off stating he was too busy to go. I parked a block away even though there was plenty of room in the lot adjoining the church. I sat in the car, watching people climbing the steps to the heavy, arched wooden doors, sometimes stopping to shake hands with one another. It looked like a tableau out of a dream of someone else's life. Tom was dead.

I sat in the truck, wondering how everyone could act as though life went on as it always had. How could they act as though everything was all right? Tom was dead.

The bells tolled ten, announcing that it was time for the service to begin. I waited until the last of the stragglers entered before making my way to the church. I walked up the six steps as I had done hundreds of times before. On this occasion, however, my legs were heavy, the colors seemed to have all faded to sepia, and the voices of the choir as I opened the door were muffled, as though my ears were stuffed with cotton. Nothing was as it should be. Tom was dead.

As the service drew to a close, and Pastor Morris was saying the benediction, I snuck out to avoid the sorrowful eyes and condolences.

Driving home, alone, in a cocoon of sadness, the words of the final hymn ran through my mind.

> *Thy saints in all this glorious war*
> *shall conquer though they die;*
> *they see the triumph from afar,*
> *by faith they bring it nigh.*
>
> *When that illustrious day shall rise,*
> *and all thy armies shine*
> *in robes of victory through the skies,*
> *the glory shall be thine.*

I had sung *Am I a Soldier of the Cross* more times than I could remember. Yet, it was the first time I had truly felt the words.

Perhaps Isaac Watts had a different message when he wrote the song centuries earlier, but for me it was a call to action against those who would harm my family, my country, and destroy my happiness. I was angry, and I was ready for someone to pay.

Other than pushing myself to work non-stop, my new-found anger didn't have an outlet. My family all gave me wide berth to sort out my emotions. But instead of relenting, my anger only intensified. I prayed to be shown how I could exact my revenge on an enemy who resided thousands of miles away.

And then, my prayers were answered. The St. Louis Post Dispatch ran an article announcing that a prisoner of war camp would be erected in the tiny hamlet of Weingarten. The town, which was home to fewer than 100 people, is about 20 miles outside Farmington. The camp was one of several to be built in the Midwest. When completed, it would house enemy soldiers captured on battlefields halfway around the world. At the bottom of the article was the sentence that told me how I could reach my enemies: 'The War Department says there will be job openings for civilians serving in a variety of capacities including secretarial...'

As soon as I was able, I applied for a position at the new camp. Even though my typing and dictation skills were a bit rusty, I got the job. I told John I wanted to go to work there, but I didn't tell him I had already been hired. We had always been a team, working together to keep the farm going, so I thought he would argue about my decision. Instead, he simply said, "If this is what you need to do, Ruth, then you should do it." Frankly, I think he was a little relieved to get me out of the house. I have to admit, I hadn't been the easiest person to live with.

That day in March when I reported for work at the camp mirrored my despair. The sky was a gloomy gray, too filled with ennui to decide if it were going to clear or rain. When I stepped off the bus, mud sucked at my feet as though great hands were reaching up to drag me down to Hell. I shrugged off my misgivings. I had come too far to give up.

After a brief orientation, the first week was spent learning our jobs and finding our way around. In just a few short months, the War Department had turned about one thousand acres of farmland into an enormous complex consisting of 380 buildings of all types including a hospital, theatre, fire station, kennels, blacksmith shop, bakery, barracks, and administration buildings. The streets that wove through the camp were paved with locally mined limestone.

I was taken aback when I saw the enormity of the project, which had been erected in such a short period.

The first prisoners arrived in early May of 1943. Ships brought the Italian soldiers from North Africa, where they had been captured. After the long, treacherous sea voyage, where there was constant fear of torpedo attacks, and overcrowding plagued the passengers, they were transported by train from Norfolk Virginia to Weingarten. When they disembarked, they marched around a half mile to the camp.

I watched to get my first glimpse of the retched men who were part of the machine of evil, threatening all that was good in the world. However, when I saw the prisoners, I was taken aback. My breath caught in my throat as I realized many of these 'men' weren't much more than children. Some, I learned later were as young as 14 when they had entered the service. I was shocked at how thin and bedraggled they were, fear clearly etched in their faces.

Maybe it was my maternal instincts, but I found myself feeling sorry for the very people whom I had wanted to punish just a few hours earlier. It's strange what happens to your soul when you see your enemy as a person not just a concept.

That night, I surprised myself when I said a prayer for the prisoners, or PWs as they were called. It was the first crack in my wall of hatred and anger, and it brought with it a wave of tears - tears I had been storing up for a very long time.

Ultimately, there were more than five thousand prisoners at the camp. In essence, we were a city. Like any city, we had our problems, but generally, things ran smoothly. Surprisingly, the Italians became an integral part of society. They were heroic in their work when the Mississippi flooded, threatening communities along the river. They helped man area farms. They held concerts for the residents and competed against local sports teams. Some were even taken by chartered bus to St. Ambrose Catholic Church, the largest Italian parish in St. Louis. Afterwards, they were treated to dinner at restaurants before being returned to the camp.

To me, the story that best illustrates how attitudes about the PWs had changed is of a work detail on the way back to the camp after a long hot day. The soldier accompanying them wanted to stop for a cold one at Midway, the neighborhood bar. Ironically, since he couldn't take his weapon inside, he left it in the truck with the men he had been assigned to guard. When he returned, his weaving gait illustrated he had had a bit too much to drink. It was obvious he couldn't safely navigate the crooked road, so one of the PWs drove home.

The prisoners had come a long way from the fearful men who had hoarded bread in their pockets in anticipation of being starved.

Most of my coworkers seemed to accept the PWs, and even care for them. However, I didn't want anything to do with them. While I had come to see them as pawns in the war, I still saw the men as somehow less human than Americans.

Unfortunately, even though I didn't want anything to do with the prisoners, with thousands of them in the camp, it was impossible to avoid them. Aldo Santo was the PW assigned to the Quartermaster's office where I worked. He helped deliver messages and ran to get documents signed and generally acted as our feet.

He was a short, young man about the same age Tom would be. His skin was tanned and his hair dark and wiry like the scrub brush I used to clean the oven. When he was being introduced, it was clear he was nervous as his eyes looked for a friendly face. I was shocked when he selected me out of the crowd. We locked eyes and each took stock of the other. I don't know what he was looking for – most likely a friend – but I was looking for a glimpse into his soul.

Evidently, what Aldo saw as he made eye contact with me was reassuring and that rocked me back on my heels. How could my enemy look me in the eye and see a friend? He had stopped the nervous rotation of his cap and he stood a little straighter, his head held high, his eyes alight with warmth. What should have made me feel better only caused me more uncertainty.

My fellow employees were thrilled to have someone happily willing to do the bothersome little tasks they didn't want to do. They had him running errands and quickly taught him how to file, although that wasn't part of his job description. You could often hear him as he and staff members tried to understand one another. Aldo's English was about as bad as our Italian. He had picked up a few words and phrases, and that was augmented with lots of pantomiming on both parts, often resulting in peals of laughter that could be heard throughout the office.

Aldo quickly became the department's mascot. He was filled with cheer incongruous as to the situation he was in. He went about his work humming a wordless tune, giving a little bob of his head when he addressed one of us. He further endeared himself to my co-workers with the daily basket of pastries he supplied. The goodies, which were made by a PW who was a chef in civilian life, were responsible for more than one expanding waistline.

For my part, I wasn't ready to give in to the young man's charms, and I resented how chummy my co-workers were getting with him.

One day, Aldo wasn't the happy-go-lucky person I had grown accustomed to. In fact, he was uncharacteristically somber. He came into my office, set some forms in my in-basket, then left without the slightest greeting. I thought it was odd but didn't give it much thought. After all, he was a prisoner being held a long way from home. Despite the relatively good life they had at the camp, it was no substitute for freedom, and all the men were susceptible to bouts of depression.

Later, I got together with several of my co-workers for lunch at the mess hall. One of the women, Lillian, asked, "Isn't it sad about Aldo?"

"It really changes your perspective when you know someone on the other side who has been hurt," said Deborah, with a sad shake of her head.

"Why, what's happened?" I asked. "I saw him earlier today. He looked blue, but I thought he was probably just suffering a bout of homesickness."

The other four looked at me as if I had horns growing out of my head. Finally, Pearl said, "Seriously? You don't know?

The town where he's from was bombed. His family's home was destroyed. His son lost an eye." She dabbed a tear from her own eye before continuing, "It is all so sad. The letter was written nearly two months ago. So, he doesn't know how they are getting by; where they are living, or anything. Poor Aldo."

I looked at my friends and it was clear they all were aware of the story, but I hadn't heard a word until just then. "Pearl, how did you know this, and I didn't? You sit right outside my door."

"Everyone knows...well, I guess everyone except you."

"How did I not know? When did you find out?" I was incredulous that everyone in my circle knew about Aldo's family, and I was in the dark.

"I guess no one thought you'd care," said Deborah, carefully avoiding eye contact with me.

"Why would you think that?" I asked looking from one to the next.

"Darling," Frank started, "it's just that we know you have your own pain to deal with..."

"What are you talking about?" I had never mentioned Tom's death at work. As far as I knew, no one was the wiser.

"Ruth, this is a small community," he continued, gently laying a hand on mine. "People talk. We figured you just needed time and when you were ready, you'd tell us yourself."

I looked around the table, and they were all nodding slightly in concurrence.

"Besides, everyone knows you hate the PWs," said Lillian.

"I don't hate them!"

"Really?" Deborah asked.

"Yes, really. Why would you say such a thing?" I demanded, my cheeks burning with a combination of embarrassment and anger. They weren't entirely wrong. I had dehumanized the PWs. Thus, I had never tried to get to know or understand any of them. I honestly didn't expect anyone to notice.

Frank looked at me long and hard before responding. "Whenever we even mention Aldo or one of the other men come in the office, you clench your jaw, and your eyes get steely and your nostrils flare. Those are all tell-tale signs of anger, you know."

"What are you some kind of dime novel detective?" I demanded. I felt my mask slipping and I needed to get away. I picked up my tray and stood to leave when Pearl put her hand on my arm to stop me.

"Please don't be mad at us, Ruth. None of us can possibly understand what you feel here surrounded by the prisoners. We worry about you, that's all."

"Well, don't. I'm fine, thank you." I turned and stalked away.

At one o'clock, when it was time to go back to work, I was feeling better. Still, I had a difficult time concentrating as a whirlwind of thoughts kept circling through my mind. I kept thinking about what Aldo must be feeling. When we had received news about Tom, I was devastated, but I had my family and my home to offer me comfort. Aldo had strangers and a prison barracks.

The next day, Aldo came to my office with some forms I needed to sign before he delivered them to the appropriate department. For the first time since I had met him, I saw him clearly. He wasn't just a foreigner in the US as punishment for being on the wrong side. He was a young man suffering. Behind his smile lay a soul that was aching with loneliness and uncertainty.

"Aldo, I heard about your son," I said, my voice sounding awkward to my own ears. "I'm so sorry. I can't imagine how difficult it must be for you to be so far from home – not being there to hold him."

Seeing the confusion on his face as he sorted through the unfamiliar words, trying to make sense of them, I smiled and said, "Tu bambino."

His face fell, tears came to his eyes. I wanted to put my arms around him in comfort but knew he could be punished with a month in the brig for such a rash action.

Instead, I clutched my hands to my heart and said, "I'm so sorry."

His wistful smile told me he understood and didn't need more words to explain.

Then, I did something I never expected to: I took the framed photo of Tom in his uniform I kept secreted in my desk drawer and handed it to him.

"You son, Missus?" he asked.

"Yes, Aldo. My son, Tom."

"He look nice." He flexed his muscles and smiled, "How you say?"

"Strong," I said with a smile.

"Strong," he repeated.

I'm not sure what he saw in my face that made his expression change and ask, "Missus? Tom, he okay?"

"No, Aldo," I whispered. My voice giving way to emotion. "No."

"I sorry, Missus."

I forced a small smile, blinking rapidly, willing back the tears, not trusting my voice to say anything more, I merely nodded my head.

After that conversation, Aldo and I had a different relationship, one built on mutual understanding and shared pain.

One day, I came into my office early in the morning to find a milk bottle serving as a vase for a bouquet of flowers. I didn't need anyone to tell me Aldo had picked them from one of the flower gardens the PWs had planted around each of the three compounds.

If there was residual anger toward those I had held responsible for Tom's death, Aldo had put it to rest. His presence in my life, despite the language barrier, had filled a hole as nothing else had.

The best way I could thank Aldo for helping me put my pain in perspective, and to apologize to him was to make the telephone calls he wasn't allowed to. With a few inquiries, I was able to get an update on his family. They and much of the rest of his village had been relocated. His son was reportedly doing well.

Before long, word got around that I could sometimes get answers, and more and more of the PWs sought me out. How could I turn my back on them? I had to try. It's what I would have hoped for my son if he were in that situation.

We became allies. Our love of family binds us together. And no one was more surprised than I was.

* * *

When the end of the war came, it was finally time for the Italians to return home. They left with many unexpected souvenirs. Some left with a greater appreciation for the United States. Some left with friendships, which would last a lifetime. Some left with new skills they learned while at the camp – skills they would take home to help rebuild their country.

At the going away party, gifts were exchanged. Frank gave Aldo a pair of binoculars, telling him, "Sell these if you need money."

Aldo grinned and said in his much-improved English, "Thank you Mr. Frank. Now I am a capitalist!"

Aldo gave me a ring he had made by melting down some of the script the PWs used in the PX. I gave him a scarf I had knit in red, green, and white, the colors of the Italian flag. I also gave him the photo of Tom. "Teach your son, Aldo."

He took the picture with reverence, and for the first time, we hugged.

* * *

After the war, I received letters from several of the men. They sent photographs of their growing families, and news of how they were enjoying civilian life. Over the years the letters became more and more infrequent except from Aldo who faithfully wrote several times a year. The first letter came about ten months after he reached his wife and son. The letter included a grainy picture of a newborn. On the back was written Tomaso Santo 26/06/1946.

As he grew, Tomaso and I became great pen pals. I was his Nonna Americana – his American Grandmother. He sent me drawings of Aldo and the rest of his family, his school and his pets. I relished each and every letter from him, and kept a scrap book of his drawings, report cards and other bits of news he and Aldo sent. He was the closest thing to a grandson I was ever going to have.

It's been almost 20 years since I received the first photograph of Tomaso. He's a man now - the same age as his namesake and father were when the war stole their youth. Fortunately, Tomaso has a different fate. John and I will soon be meeting him for the first time when he arrives in St. Louis, where he will study at Washington University. He wants to learn to build bridges. I suspect that his desired career path was inspired by the metaphorical bridges his father built during his time as a PW.

The years since Tom died have dulled the pain. More often than not, thoughts of him bring smiles rather than tears. I miss him every day, and I'll never understand those who choose war. But I'm eternally grateful for the gift I was given. When I prayed for revenge, God gave me love in the form of Aldo and the others I once saw as my enemy – a love that saved my soul and freed my heart. A love that brought me peace.

The Moon on the Water

A.L. Butcher

Flowing down the looming edifices of the Jagged Peak Mountains, which cross the land of Erana, are many waterfalls. The snows last long and the springtime comes late but when it does the waters run fast and clear, roaring their song among the echoing peaks. Such a song it is that once when the world was young a goddess stopped to listen. Shadows are plenty among the peaks, and caves even more so, and it is in these dark places the waters pool, cold and still, mirroring the glittering darkness. She stood in the first nights of the world and reached to touch the image of the moon on the water, reflected through a crack in the rocks.

Many creatures were born when the magic was wild and free. Guardians of the wild places they would become, and when there were mortals to believe they would become gods; for those whose lives end often seek out those who endure. Acionna had been born of the rock, the water and the snow. She was a child of all and none, a child of the raw magic of the earth and streams. So it was the elemental walked among the rock and water, a goddess of sorts.

Hair the colour of snow flowed like the froth on the water, curling around a face as dark of hue as the rocks from which the mountains were born; blue-black with a touch of silver, which sparkled in the morning sun. She was the essence of the mountain, and the midnight sky. Wide eyes of opal and sapphire, bright and shining, both young as the springtime and old as the rocks looked out upon the world. Her clothes were none, for it is only mortals who feel shame. Mountains care not for nakedness and so she moved among the rocks with nothing upon her skin save the rain and the mist from the water.

So, it was when the springtime brought the melts and the rain, and the waters in the caverns and waterfalls roared a he-troll of the tribe of Var ventured far from his regular lands. Hirik was he, a shape-shifter of the warrior caste. In these days long ago, before the Plague ravaged the land, and its pernicious fingers touched even the mountain folk the trolls held the knowledge of transmogrification and he could soar as an eagle, run the paths as a wolf or scramble between rocks as a bear. In latter days they could assume but one form but in the young days of the world the magic was theirs to tame as they chose. Those who held the Relic of the Moon commanded the most complex magic, for they could turn flesh to fire, water, wood or stone, they could see threads of the future weaved like cloth and perhaps, if they were skilled enough, could understand what they saw.

Magic has its price and that price was war. Other tribes coveted the Relic, gift of the Lady of the Sky, and so fought the tribes of the Jagged Peaks, staining the rock with blood and even poisoning the streams. In the infancy of the world, the mortal races were young and foolish. Some remained so.

The troll, Talin Var, was out alone, scouting on the trails left by his enemies, the Sal. They were crafty; they used any means they could to bring foul sickness, to bring wicked magic and bloody mayhem to their foes. If he could find where they hid, their stores and their caches then perhaps the Var could even the odds.

Far from home was this troll, but trolls fear little and he drew his fine axe, forged from the bronze mined beneath the mountains. The edge was sharp, and his skill even sharper. Troll women could fight as well as their men and he thought, perhaps this was another of his enemies, perhaps a Shaman or a sorceress as he saw no weapon beneath the flowing hair. Then she spun about and the troll almost dropped his axe. She was naked and seemed not to mind this fact and about her was a glow, the soft light of magic. Talin stood mesmerised; she was enchanting, like the mountains and the waterfall. He had never seen one such as Acionna. Hers was an earthy beauty with hips a man just wanted to slide his hands across, curvaceous and broad. Although he tried to stop himself the troll's eyes roamed her body, from the face with its look of timeless innocence to the curve of her breasts. He thought to say something but just mumbled incoherently. Acionna smiled and Talin was lost.

Atop a rock, on a bed of moss, they made love, the goddess and the warrior. She had never loved before, and the heady emotions brought such ecstasy, such delight to the lonely goddess of the mountain. Beneath a waterfall, he took her, with the water roaring past them. In a cave filled with crystals which glittered like stars, she took him, their cries echoing about them. He had never been loved with such passion, and his heart was entirely hers. War was but a memory when they lay together.

War did not know this, and battle will be fought when it chooses. Trolls, elves and men are but its creatures. The war continued, month after bloody month, and neither side prevailed. With battle came those things which walk alongside war – disharmony, chaos and hatred. It took much persuasion and whispered entreaties in the passion of lovemaking to convince Acionna to fight for the Var. When gods become involved in war the odds are unfair and a price must surely be paid, but from whom is never clear.

Acionna held the wild magic, the primal Power, the very essence of sorcery and for the sake of her lover and his tribe she brought it to bear upon those they fought. From her fingers ran the torrents of the mountain, fierce and unyielding as they swept away the enemies. Sal trolls grabbed at rocks or thrust their weapons into the ground to no avail as warriors were swept over crevasses and into the hard rock walls. The ground beneath her enemies rippled and cracked, tumbling warriors and unsettling their battle beasts.

The Sal fielded greater numbers; their tribe spanned many settlements and their Shaman had learned the secrets of the dark fae magic, traded for gold, prisoners of war and for blood. The warriors of the tribe of Var were pushed back, and the rocks were stained red with blood as the sickness swept their ranks. Blood poured from eyes and mouths, drenching everything about them. Twisting tendrils of magic grabbed at throats like unseen hands, choking away life and squeezing out hope. The dead rose on feet of bone, in the days before the trolls burned their dead and limbs hacked from torsos leapt, kicking, scratching, blinding until the trolls of Varris trembled. Their Shaman Lirana called the magic from the Relic of the Moon as her sight faded from eyes pulled from her face by the hands of the dead and her throat constricted with the dark, curse magic of her foes. The death-words of a Shaman carry much Power and the magic flowed with her blood to turn the attackers before her to stone; statues now diving forward in attack, and one with a stone arm clutched about the neck of a dying troll Shaman. With their Shaman slain, the Var were demoralised, yet fought for their own survival as the Relic rolled from the hands of their queen.

Diving forward Hirik warrior Orlin Sal snatched the Relic of the Moon and raised it high; the victory chant of his tribe echoed among the towering peaks, a thunderous cacophony roaring among the paths and trails. The Relic soon reached their Shaman, who laughed and motioned her troops onwards. It was not enough to possess the Relic of the Moon, she wished to kill or enslave her enemies. More slaves bought her more magic, more wealth and more status. More blood could be traded with the fae. She had heard the words and seen the tendrils of magic from the previous owner and cried her own. Pouring forth like a torrent with the twisted darkness of the magic she held the Power turned her most of her kin and some of her foes to nought but statues. Frozen and fixed in rock and in time. Magic demands a price and on that plain of war, that price was the lives and the futures of those who fought. Magic is fickle. Magic is wild and magic may be a blessing and it may be a curse.

Talin, at the fore of the battle, and whose axe was stained crimson with Sal blood turned to stare back at his goddess atop a rock, her name on his lips as the stone crawled up his legs, along his arms; bone and flesh became stone. Thus, was he fixed, and in times to come would be known as the Talinstone. In her grief and her rage, Acionna roared like the waterfalls she loved, and her magic scourged the rocks until the blood mixed with stone to fuse in the veins which would later mark the mountains; the veins of ruby and bloodstone. What was done could not be undone on that day as the Relic tumbled into the darkness of the mountain caves. Her grief and revenge were terrible, and those who had been spared ran for their lives as rock fell and water poured from fissures and split the ground. The very Jagged Peaks tottered and trembled; the plateau of war cracked until none could pass, and statues tumbled to lie beneath the clear but steaming waters of the new lake. It would be known as the Lake of Blood.

The Varris, such as they were fled to the north, across the bridge of ice and made a new life, mourning their dead and their goddess; paying homage for their sins to the Lady of the Skies and the waterfalls and rock-pools. They searched for the Relic, but dared not risk the Dark Paths, where the Realms of Magic leech into the mundane realm and strange creatures walk. The Sal ran to the east and as no children were born to the tribe their numbers dwindled. Their name became a pariah and they memory tarnished with shame. When a goddess seeks revenge it surely comes, and it comes in many forms. The dark and forbidden magic fell when the Sal fell and never again did the trolls of that region trade with the fae. Magic demands a price and often cares not who pays it.

Acionna herself wandered among the dark, and shadowy places as her child-belly grew, and at the edge of a pool in which the moon shone reflected she birthed a daughter, Sendrillia, who was neither troll nor goddess but a little of each. And so, despite her grief she was not alone. The Relic of the Moon became a myth, a symbol of the past, as did all the Relics when the magic waned and hid its face from the Plague and the sight of the Witch-Hunters who hate it so. Misremembered and misunderstood it settled in a cave, deep and dark. If there were any to look upon the still lake in the cave filled with crystals, they would see a disk as round and pale as the moon on the water. For its light flickered and ebbed but did not die.

Postcard to the Bomb Shelter Babies

Colene Allen

"Ukrainian mothers give birth in bomb shelters" - CBS News, March 3/2022

"To be, or not to be: that is the question:" is the age old query posed by the doomed Hamlet in William Shakespeare's famous play. Hamlet's infamous utterance was a contemplation of the meaning of his existence and an internal debate about whether life or death is better.

A few weeks ago, Ukrainian President Volodomyr Zelenskyy invoked that famous line in an address to the Parliament of the United Kingdom. For Zelenskyy and Ukraine, it's not a question at all. They fully intend to continue being.

On November 3rd and 4th, 1940, German Forces carried out two bombing raids against the port city of Aberdeen in northern Scotland. History records Aberdeen as being the most frequently bombed city in Britain between 1940 and 1943, in total amounting to 34 bombing raids. Across Scotland, more than 2,500 people were killed during over 500 bombing raids.

Jane (Jenny) Matheson Freeland was born in Aberdeen on April 5, 1909. In 1939, she married a Canadian Paratrooper enlisted in the Royal Air Force, and by the time the Germans began their bombing raids in Aberdeen, she was pregnant with their first child. At full term and ready to give birth any day, Jenny was forced into a bomb shelter those two days in November of 1940, not knowing she would go into labour and give birth to her daughter as the Germans rained bombs down on the city she called home. With none of the reassuring comforts of a hospital or medical staff to assist her and the sirens wailing as explosions shook the ground underneath her, Jenny brought her daughter into a world full of turmoil, tragedy, and death. It was a world that would not see an end to the violence, trauma, destruction, and death of World War Two until five years later.

Incredibly, and against all the odds, Jenny and her daughter survived all 34 bombing raids carried out by the Germans between 1940 and 1943. In 1946, they accompanied Jenny's husband Bill back to Canada, where they settled into post-war life. The small family expanded to include a son born in Canada in 1947. Bill died in 1972, with Jenny waiting until 1989 to be reunited with him. The daughter that was born in the bomb shelter passed away in 2020, and their son is the only one of the original family still alive. Jenny's daughter had two children of her own – a daughter followed five years later by a son.

Jenny Freeland was my grandmother. The daughter born in the bomb shelter was my mother. I exist despite every attempt by a foreign military force to try and erase my grandmother, my mother, and myself.

The headlines in media around the world touting the birth of children in the bomb shelters and subway tunnels of Ukraine aren't beacons of hope for me, nor are they a cause to rejoice. Those headlines are a stark reminder of my family history, and cause a feeling of rage that I can't find a way to justify or express.

Wisdom of the ancients calls it "blood memory", and another theory is a genetic imprint. Regardless of what it's called, the reality is that were it not for a twist of lucky fate, I may have never even existed. I may have never been conceived, born, or had a chance to breathe on this planet. That sounds rather dramatic, I grant you. However, that doesn't change how true that reality is, or how much it leads to the big question of my purpose and existence.

I had the privilege of knowing my grandmother for the first twenty years of my life. Jenny was true to her heritage, being a full-blooded member of the Matheson Highland Clan. They didn't come more stubborn, determined, opinionated, or strong of mind and body than my grandmother. I received more than one tirade from her in Gaelic when I was young for doing something she was unimpressed with. She would go off on me in Gaelic, a language I didn't understand at all, and it was best to just hang my head low until she finished. After she stopped yelling, I would look up carefully and sheepishly at her and just tell her "I ken, Granny. I ken. I'ma sorry."

That my grandmother was strong enough to survive giving birth to a child in a bomb shelter, as the enemy dropped bombs all around her, doesn't surprise me. That she survived the significant number of air raids the Germans carried out on Aberdeen, however, is shocking. In the impersonal and deadly arena of war, the Germans certainly had the opportunity many times to eliminate my entire family line. They failed, much to my amazement and joy.

My mother, Sylvia, passed away on May 1st, 2020 of complications from Diabetes. I doubt she had any recollection of the circumstances of her birth beyond the bare facts. I had heard the 'family legend' that she was born during an air raid many times, and had written it off as an inside joke. It was at my mother's funeral that my uncle confirmed the story as true and fact. That simple confirmation explained much about the woman who was my biggest supporter and best friend in life.

Sylvia was also true to her Scottish Highlander heritage. She was equal in stubbornness to her own mother, albeit with a rather blunted edge. She was not quick to anger, but when Mom was angry, EVERYONE knew it. She had perfected what we now call the 'side-eye' glance long before it was trendy, and was a master at getting her children to self-confess their sins. Mom was charming, endearing, and lived a life full of rich relationships and wonderfully powerful and inspiring connections and moments.

Without my mother, a small collection of young men here in Canada would never have had the opportunities to meet their heroes as they battled cancer or tried to adjust to their new reality of living with Diabetes. She wasn't an activist with a loud mouth. She quietly went about the business of making things happen to improve the lives of others by giving of herself again and again. Her devotion to service in her immediate community and those outside of it was a value that she left to me to carry on. My mother was strong, both in character and personality. She was a force of nature to be reckoned with when you fell on her bad side, and your greatest ally when you fell on her good side.

Had my grandmother and mother been killed by a German bomb during those two days of air raids on their home, you would not be reading these words right now. I would never have existed. At all.

There are some people who would rejoice at hearing I was nearly wiped out of existence. There are others who would lament the lack of my presence. I really don't care about my detractors. They don't matter. I do care about my supporters, because I would like to think that I have made their lives better by being here. It's very possible my punching out the teenager in high school that was bullying my good friend with Cerebral Palsy was one of those rare moments that explains my existence. The three generations of women in my family must have been saved from those bombs for a reason.

In my life, which is far from over, I have accomplished a few things. I've helped people to find employment, taught people with physical challenges how to use computers, and co-founded a Community Garden in my neighbourhood. I volunteered hundreds of hours to Food Banks, the Canadian Mental Health Association, and am a staunch advocate for the homeless and those challenged by mental health issues. I have written for newspapers, have a partial manuscript on my laptop hard drive for a non-fiction book at life in a ground-breaking prototype homeless shelter program, and spend my time telling people with substance use challenges that I'm going to give them hell if I ever hear them refer to themselves as 'junkies' again. I have saved lives, supported the forgotten, and tried to take the small victories as a motivator to keep moving forward.

Is there a point in all of this rambling on? My hope is that one day, one of the children born in those bomb shelters and subway tunnels in Ukraine during this terrible war will have the chance to read my words and understand my existential dilemma. I would like to think that the families that survive this war through the trial of fire of being born during a bombing raid will be able to move forward with strength and the conviction that they and their lineage exist because the world still needs them. And to their children, who would be my peers in this unbelievable war, I can only say that it's useless to question luck or existence, although it appears to be unavoidable in my case.

What does matter is what we do with the life we have. In my case, I'm trying to live up to the legacy of having been saved for a reason. After all, my contribution to this anthology may be the reason my grandmother, my mother, and I were all saved.

I plan to live in gratitude for my existence, not in conflict with the circumstances that nearly stole my life before it began. I've realized that we're all here to experience the good and the bad, the happy and the sad, the wondrous and the monstrous. It is the nature of fate and life to be balanced between the light and the darkness. The darkness wins when it gets the chance to creep into our souls and take away the light. Living in gratitude brings the light back into the dark places in my soul. I work to be grateful for all the opportunities I've had to make changes in the lives of others. I'm grateful for the opportunity to wake up early some mornings and watch the sun rise while sipping a tea. I look for beauty, meaning, and the silver linings in each moment and each life event.

Above all else, I love.

If the death and devastation that we're seeing waged in Eastern Europe is to end, we need to love. Without hesitation, reservation, or fear. Without malice, vengeance, or anger.

We must not forget to love.

The children born in the bomb shelters in Ukraine deserve this much from us for their terrifying entry into this world.

They deserve our love.

Always Read the Fine Print

Joe Bonadonna

When timid little Debbie was ten years old, she discovered that monsters lived in her closet and under her bed. Although they never bothered her, always sticking to the shadows but always watching her, she was still frightened by this discovery. She complained to her parents over and over again, but they didn't believe her, never once checked her closet or under her bed, and just told her to do her homework and stop making up stories and acting like a big baby.

Debbie soon grew resentful of her parents and thought they were very mean. One evening, after once again telling them that she had seen the monsters, they beat her and then sent her to bed without her supper. They also grounded her for a month: no TV, no books, no movies, no music, no internet, and no texting or phone calls to and from her friends. After school each day she had to report straight home and stay in her room until supper time; they gave her only moldy bread and dirty, warm water to eat and drink. After supper, she had to go back to her room to study, study, study. Even her bratty little brother told her there were no such things as monsters, and he laughed at her and made fun of her. He often bullied and hit her, even though he was a year younger and somewhat smaller. Their parents never punished him.

While she lay in bed crying her heart out that night, one monster emerged from her closet and another crawled out from under her bed to speak with her. Frightened though she may have been, there was darkness in Debbie's soul that aroused her curiosity and fascination, and was surely the reason the monsters had moved into her room in the first place.

"We know your pain and frustration, Debbie," said one monster who looked like an alligator crossed with a lobster, "and we are here to help you."

Debbie wiped the tears from her eyes. "But how? How can you help me?"

"We can remedy your situation," said the second monster; this one was a werewolf with long, sharp claws, large and glistening fangs, and four arms. "We can teach you magic and how to use it, and no one will ever bully you or make fun of you again."

"I don't understand. How can you help me?" Debbie asked.

"Serve us," said the first monster, "and we, in turn, will serve you."

"Just give us permission to do what we came here to do," the werewolf told her.

Debbie didn't have to think twice about this. The thought of learning magic and how to use it was very much to her liking. "What do you want from me?"

So, the monsters told her what they wanted her to do and thus she all too quickly gave them the permission they required from her.

"Now what?" she asked.

"You must sign an exclusive contract with us," the monsters said in unison.

Debbie was only too happy to comply.

That night, Debbie's mother and father learned there were indeed monsters living in their daughter's closet and under her bed when she gave the monsters permission to eat her parents. For dessert, she told the demonic duo that it was okay for them to go ahead and eat her bratty little brother, too.

After that, the monsters took Debbie away to their secret Shadowland, from where they controlled the kings and queens, and the politicians and wealthy captains of industry who held all the power on Earth. But the monsters pulled all the strings: they were the puppet masters who truly ruled the world in secret, but keeping always to the dark corners of our world.

As the years went by and Debbie learned all about magic, she used her powers to corrupt the politicians and religious leaders, the military elite and all the rulers in the world, just as the monsters told her to do. And as her powers and influence over the Earth grew, she caused wars, famine, plagues and natural disasters, and steered the course of human events in any direction that suited her whims. Over and over again she would select people she thought would be a wonderful snack for her two monstrous benefactors, and they devoured these individuals with great relish. The monsters were most pleased with Debbie and her work, and she continued to serve them well.

However, as Debbie's powers grew stronger over the passing of time, the monsters began to fear her, and they grew more and more concerned about their own well-being. They were afraid that the darkness in Debbie's soul, which gave her so much joy over causing all the havoc and turmoil in the world, would one day expose their secret and drag them out of the shadows of our world. They feared that Debbie would turn on them and destroy them.

One day, the monsters of Shadowland decided they had to act immediately, before it was too late. Thus, on her thirtieth birthday, the monsters called Debbie to a conference.

"Now, while you have served us well over the years and provided us with many tasty snacks, your actions and your growing power are most troublesome to us," said the alligator-lobster hybrid. "We believe you have overstepped your bounds and can no longer be trusted."

"Therefore," said the four-armed werewolf, "we have no choice but to invoke Article 13 of the contract you signed with us twenty years ago."

Debbie was confused and surprised. "Article 13? What's that?"

"You mean to say you never read that clause in the contract? You never read the fine print?" asked the first monster.

"But no one told me to! I was just a child at the time!" Debbie said. "What's this clause you're talking about?"

"Simply put," said monster #1, cleaning his lobster claws. "Article 13 gives us the power to punish you and take away your magic, should you ever step out of line. We have decided your services are no longer required."

"Punish me? How?" Debbie asked, growing frightened, something she hadn't experienced since the night the monsters first spoke to her. She knew that her magic had no power over the monsters. "What sort of power does that contract give you?"

Monster #2 bared his glistening fangs. "The power of attorney."

And with that, the two monsters gobbled Debbie up, bones and all.

"Quite a nice little snack, don't you think?" asked the first monster, his alligator jaws opened wide in a long, drawn-out yawn.

The four-armed werewolf licked his fangs. "Indeed so," he agreed. "Debbie should have hired an attorney. Karma, as they say, is a real bitch."

Yes, indeed it is. For what goes around eventually comes around.

I should know. I'm one of the monsters.

Meet the Authors

Colene Allen is a retired freelance writer from Ontario, Canada. She wrote non-fiction articles for The Toronto Star, P1 Magazine, and other publications in the motorsports industry. Allen's other areas of work include domestic and international law, human rights, mental health, and homelessness.

Joe Bonadonna is the author of the heroic fantasies Mad Shadows—Book One: The Weird Tales of Dorgo the Dowser (winner of the 2017 Golden Book Readers' Choice Award for Fantasy); Mad Shadows—Book Two: The Order of the Serpent; Mad Shadows—Book Three: The Heroes of Echo Gate; the space opera Three Against The Stars and its sequel, the sword and planet space adventure, The MechMen of Canis-9; and the sword & sorcery pirate novel, Waters of

Darkness, in collaboration with David C. Smith. With co-writer Erika M Szabo, he penned Three Ghosts in a Black Pumpkin (winner of the 2017 Golden Books Judge's Choice Award for Children's Fantasy), and its sequel, The Power of the Sapphire Wand.

In addition to his fiction, Joe has written numerous articles, book reviews and author interviews for Black Gate online magazine.

A. L. Butcher is an award-winning author of dark fantasy, historical fantasy, short stories and poetry. With a background in classics, mythology, politics and creative writing her eclectic affinities bring an alchemical flair to her work. Based in the South West UK she enjoys her garden, nature, literature and losing herself in a myriad world of words.

J.C. Fields is a multi-award-winning and Amazon bestselling author. His Sean Kruger Series has won numerous medals in the annual Readers' Favorite International Book Awards. Plus, his first book in his Michael Wolfe Saga, A Lone Wolf, became a #1 Best Selling audiobook in March of 2020.

As one of the featured authors on the highly successful YouTube podcast, Fear From the Heartland, hosted by Paul J. McSorley, he offers a variety of original short stories penned specifically for its listeners.

He is active in numerous writers' groups and serves on the board of Sleuths' Ink Mystery Writers. He is also a full member of the Missouri Writers' Guild.

He lives with his wife, Connie, in Southwest Missouri.

Inge-Lise Goss, USA Today, Award-Winning Best Selling author, was born in Denmark, raised in Utah, and now lives in the foothills of Red Rock Canyon with her husband and their dog, Ted. She spends most of her time in her den writing stories. There, with her muse by her side, her imagination has no boundaries, and her dreams come alive. When she's not pounding away on the keyboard, she can be found reading, rowing, or trying to perfect her golf game, which she fears is a lost cause.

Richard Groller is an author of fiction and non-fiction. He is co-author of The Warrior's Edge and a contributing author to The American Warrior. Nominated for Military Intelligence Professional Writer of the Year in 1986, he has published numerous historical and technical articles in such venues as Military Intelligence, The Field Artillery Journal, Guns and Ammo, and the Journal of Electronic Defense, and has been cited as the primary source for sections of several textbooks on Electronic Warfare. A member of both SFWA, HWA and SFPA, Rich has been published in 6 Volumes of the Heroes of Hell shared universe anthology and the horror anthology What Scares the Boogeyman? He has been published in 4 volumes of the Sha'Daa: Tales of the Apocalypse series, and is Editor of The Book of Night, an illustrated book of macabre poetry, He is also published in 2 horror anthologies Terror By Gaslight and Dark Corners. He has been published in 2 bestselling HWA Horror Poetry Showcases, Volumes III and IV.

Michael H. Hanson created the ongoing SHA'DAA shared-world anthology series currently consisting of "SHA'DAA: TALES OF THE APOCALYPSE", "SHA'DAA: LAST CALL", "SHA'DAA: PAWNS," "SHA'DAA: FACETS", "SHA'DAA: INKED", "SHA'DAA: TOYS," and "SHA'DAA: ZOMBIE PARK", all published by Moondream Press. Michael's short story "C.H.A.D." appears in the Crystal Lake Publishing anthology "C.H.U.D. LIVES!", his short story "Rock and Road" appears in the Roger Zelazny tribute anthology "SHADOWS AND REFLECTIONS," his short story "Born Of Dark Waters" appears in the Independent Legions Publishing anthology "THE BEAUTY OF DEATH 2: DEATH BY WATER," and his short story "Night Shopper" appears in William Morrow Paperbacks' "OTHER TERRORS: An Inclusive Anthology." Michael has stories in Janet Morris's Heroes in Hell (HIH) anthology volumes, "LAWYERS IN HELL," "ROGUES IN HELL,"

"DREAMERS IN HELL," "POETS IN HELL," "DOCTORS IN HELL," "PIRATES IN HELL," "LOVERS IN HELL," "MYSTICS IN HELL." and "LIARS IN HELL." Michael has written and sold over 100 short stories in the fields of science fiction, fantasy, and horror. He also has penned and had published six poetry collections "AUTUMN BLUSH," "JUBILANT WHISPERS," "WHEN THE NIGHT OWL SCREAMS," "DARK PARCHMENTS," "ANDROID GIRL," and "QUARANTINE WORLD."

Rebecca Lacy's passion for writing was awakened when she was still in elementary school. However, it got pushed aside for more 'sensible' endeavors as an adult. Thankfully, she outgrew adulthood!

That was like a butterfly being released from her cocoon, and the love of creating was reawakened. Since then, she has contributed short stories to several anthologies, and has co-authored a business fable, "Leadership in Wonderland."

She is currently working on two novels. *The Women Who Loved Tom Monroe*, is an historical novel, set in southeast Missouri during WWII. The second is a spirited multigenerational look at the relationships between mothers and daughters. She also has a collection of short, short stories, which will soon be published.

Rebecca writes in a variety of genres – vacillating between children's, business, mystery, historical fiction, and fantasy, or whatever else strikes her fancy on any given day.

Vickie Johnstone lives in London, UK, and has self-published 17 books. She works as a sub-editor. She loves reading, writing, films, the sea, art, animals (especially cats), nature, rock music and travelling. Her books are mainly fantasy, and include a series for children about a magical cat, an adult zombies series, a YA fantasy adventure, a comedy detective series for YA, a romcom starring a talking dog and poetry.

Cat series: *Kiwi in Cat City, Kiwi and the Missing Magic, Kiwi and the Living Nightmare, Kiwi and the Serpent of the Isle, Kiwi in the Realm of Ra*, and *Kiwi's Christmas Tail.*

Poetry: *Kaleidoscope, Travelling Light, Life's Rhythms, Mind-spinning Rainbows* and *A Poem a Day.*

Comedy: *Day of the Living Pizza* and *Day of the Pesky Shadow* (Smarts & Dewdrop Mysteries.

Romcom: *3 Heads and a Tail.*

Fantasy adventure: *The Sea Inside.*

Zombies: *I Dream of Zombies* and *Haven.*

Rebecca Miller's writing credits include being a freelance journalist for The Inquisitr, The Weekly Register-Call, The Daily Camera, and the Earthkeeper. I also did transcription work for President Obama.

She live's in Denver, Colorado and works as adjunct faculty for my local community college teaching nursing arts, anatomy and physiology, and medical terminology. Writing is my side job while I'm on sabbatical.

Marta Moran Bishop - I walk in the shoes of my characters and weave the tapestry of their lives with the thread of my dreams.

In my stories when I walk in another's shoes I accept the cloak of their life experiences, if only for a moment, I feel the depth of them. Their pain, sorrow, joys, & magic. It opens my eyes to their plight & I learn something different about myself and others.

I am a multi-genre author who loves to write in first person, be it animal or human. Though when finished the stories or poems of my grandmother, mother, or sister, many times I had to switch to second or third person in order to write in their voice, thus finishing the story.

I love reading, writing, riding my horses, and all animals.

Historical fiction author, **Sean Poage,** has had an exciting and varied life, as a laborer, salesman, soldier, police officer, investigator, computer geek and author. A history buff his entire life, he is most drawn to the eras of the ancient Greeks and Dark Ages Britain. Travelling the world to see history up close is his passion.

Rhavensfyre is the pen name of east coast writer KL. She and her spouse live on a small farm with a small herd of horses, two dogs and several cats in tow. In their spare time, they try to keep an organic garden and enjoy the fact that their farm is also home to several owls, a pair of hawks, and one annoying woodpecker. In addition to the living creatures, KL enjoys cycling and anything that takes her out into nature. In her spare time she researches the best ways to survive the inevitable zombie apocalypse

Anthea Sharp - Discover more from USA Today bestselling fantasy author Anthea Sharp at www.antheasharp.com, plus join her mailing list, where you'll get another Celtic fairy tale free just for signing up! Anthea Sharp's Newsletter (subscribepage.com)

Andrew P. Weston is a bestselling author from the UK who lives with a large amount of rescue cats in a medium sized house on a small Greek island. As well as suffering from an inordinate compulsion to make things up and write them down for other peoples' entertainment, he is also an expert nuisance . . . just ask his wife.

Diana L. Wicker is an indie author living in the balmy climate of the US south with her family and fur babies (two dogs and two cats). She enjoys working backstage for her children's dance productions, sewing, cosplay, and customizing Asian ball jointed dolls to into characters from Feyron and other tales.

Charles Yallowitz was born, raised, and educated in New York. Then he spent a few years in Florida, realized his fear of alligators, and moved back to the Empire State. When he isn't working hard on his epic fantasy stories, Charles can be found cooking or going on whatever adventure his son has planned for the day. Truthfully, his tales of adventure are much more interesting than his real life, so skip the bio and dive into the action.

Victoria Zigler is a blind vegan poet and children's author. Born and raised in the shadow of the Black Mountains of Wales, UK, she moved away from Wales three times: once to spend six months living in Alberta, Canada, the other times to spend a few years living near Hastings on the South-East coast of England, UK, each time returning to Wales. Now she lives in Wales again, along with a chinchilla named Mollie, a West Highland White Terrier named Lilie, a Cavapoo named Logan, a Hermann's Tortoise named Artemis, and her Canadian husband, Kelly.

Printed in Poland
by Amazon Fulfillment
Poland Sp. z o.o., Wrocław
29 May 2022